CROWN OF CREATION

A BIBLE STUDY SERIES

WOMEN
OF THE
GENESIS

CINDY COLLEY

Books with Class

PUBLISHING DESIGNS, INC.

P.O. Box 3241 • Huntsville, Alabama 35810
256-533-4301 • www.publishingdesigns.com

Publishing Designs, Inc.
P.O. Box 3241
Huntsville, Alabama 35810

Poems by author unless otherwise noted.

All scripture quotations are from the New King James Version unless otherwise noted.

2nd Printing, 2009

Library of Congress Cataloging-in-Publication Data

Colley, Cindy, 1959-
        Women of the Genesis / Cindy Colley.
        p. cm.--(Crown of creation)
Includes bibliographical references and index.
ISBN 0-929540-48-4 (alk. paper)
1. Women in the Bible--Textbooks. 2. Bible. O.T. Genesis--
Textbooks. 3. Christian women--Religious life--Textbooks. I.
Title. II. Series.

BS575.C547 2005
222'.110922'082--dc22
2005000067

Printed in the United States of America

This book is lovingly dedicated to my mother, Mrs. Johnnia Duncan Holder,

whose ideals and influence permeate its pages and become more evident

in my life with the passing of each day.

With special thanks to my husband, Glenn, who inspires, encourages,

and enriches me each day toward greater service in the kingdom.

CONTENTS

INTRODUCTION

The importance of the role of women in God's Word cannot be over-estimated. Similarly, the influence of the twenty-first century woman is felt in the pulse of nations as she, through the home and the children she nurtures, weaves the moral fiber of generations to come. A study of the books of Kings and Chronicles bears out the impact of motherhood on the fate of nations. Often the Old Testament reveals the character of a king just before or just after stating the identity of his mother. Familiar examples include Joash in 2 Chronicles 24:1–2; Josiah in 2 Kings 22:1–2; and Hezekiah in 2 Chronicles 29:1–2. From this we see the power of the lives of the women of the Bible.

God, in His infinite wisdom, has pictured for us every type of woman in any society. We see all classes, from the poverty-stricken widow with only two mites, to the lavishly wealthy queen of Sheba. We see women of all ages, various lifestyles, and with every problem common to us today. We watch them conquering against immeasurable odds, and we see them tragically crushed by the tempter. They show us the beauty of holiness and the loathsome nature of sin. *Women of the Genesis* is all about the universal truths of life, as relevant today as in the Garden of Eden or on the Plains of Mamre.

As contemporary women, it behooves us to give prayerful and careful study to the lives of these women of yesterday—their victories and defeats, their virtues and vices—that from them we might gain wisdom in the directing of our own lives. "Now all these things happened to them as examples, and they were written for our admonition, upon whom the ends of the ages have come" (1 Corinthians 10:11).

All scripture quotations are from the New King James Version unless otherwise noted.

CHAPTER 1

PARADISE LOST

EVE

EVE

Eve, the mother of all living, was the only woman ever to live in a world unmarred by the presence of sin. Every true joy imaginable to woman was a reality for Eve in the Garden of Eden. Likewise, every sorrow woman knows had its ruinous beginning in the same garden as Eve tasted the poison of sin and death.

EVE'S CREATION (GENESIS 2:20–22; 3:20)

When Adam carried out his God-given task of naming all the animals of God's creation, it became evident that there was a loneliness within man that could not be pacified by any of the creatures created thus far. Genesis 2:20 actually means that there was no helper "worthy of a man."

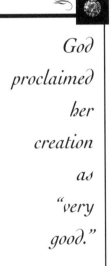

God proclaimed her creation as "very good."

The crown of God's creation at this time was man, created in the image of God Himself. It is gratifying to realize that even this man, to whom was given dominion over all the earth, was incomplete without woman. God must have intended for woman to wield a powerful influence over His creation, for it was only after her creation that He could proclaim His finished product "very good" (Genesis 1:31).

A woman is that special and final creation of God, designed to fill a void in humanity that nothing else could fill. She is the glory of the man (1 Corinthians 11:7). The fact that she was formed from the very bone of the man shows that she is not of inferior substance. It also shows the truest of kinship between man and woman. She is bone of his bones and flesh of his flesh. It is interesting to notice that woman was not formed from the foot of man as to be beneath him. Nor was she formed from his head to be superior. Some have considered the rib symbolic of the equality of worth in man and woman. Even though God established different roles for the two sexes, He in no way assigned more worth to either.

It is interesting to note at this point that those who espouse the theory of organic evolution are at a complete loss when attempting to explain the origin of females. Only creationists can account for the existence of the second sex.

Discuss how a woman is a helper "worthy" or "suitable" for a man?

physically _____

emotionally_____

spiritually _____

Find a New Testament passage indicating that husbands should honor their wives.

_____

Have a class member go to apologeticspress.org and research the origin of the female sex. Have the researcher bring quotes and other materials from evolutionists to be used for class discussion.

THE FIRST MARRIAGE (GENESIS 2:24–25)

With the creation of Eve complete, God gave her to the man, instituting and approving the state of marriage. Thus, as God gives the first bride in marriage, we read Adam's first recorded words: "This is now bone of my bones and flesh of my flesh; she shall be called Woman, because she was taken out of Man" (Genesis 2:23).

Adam recognized the woman as a priceless, God-given gift. She was perfectly designed to meet his every need. Her character was to fill his emotional void of loneliness and her body was specifically built to satisfy his physical needs. How perfect was God's plan for woman! "Therefore a man shall leave his father and mother and be joined to his wife, and they shall become one flesh" (Genesis 2:24).

These words show the intention of God that people, throughout the ages, be united in marriage. Here we find the first emphasis on leaving father and mother. God still requires this exclusive commitment in marriage (Matthew 19:5).

Why do you think God emphasized leaving before cleaving?

_____

Discuss the newness of some of Eve's circumstances. (Example: She delivered a child having never seen a human birth.) Do you think God helped prepare her for these life surprises? Could her inexperience have contributed to her vulnerability to Satan? Discuss.

SEVEN FALLS OF EVE (GENESIS 3:1–7)

The first sin, as most sin is today, was a progressive response to a calculated temptation of Satan. Notice from Genesis 3 and from the additional passages below the mistakes Eve made in this historic fall. Are we much as Eve was in our progressive entanglement in sin?

1. She listened (John 8:44).
2. She looked (1 Thessalonians 5:22).
3. She desired (Romans 12:9).
4. She took (1 John 3:4).
5. She tempted someone else (Romans 14:13).
6. She hid (Psalm 69:5).
7. She blamed someone else (Romans 14:10–12).

Which of Eve's seven falls do you think was most damaging? Why?

_____

THE WAY OF ESCAPE

No temptation has overtaken you except such as is common to man; but God is faithful, who will not allow you to be tempted beyond what you are able, but with the temptation will also make the way of escape, that you may be able to bear it (1 Corinthians 10:13).

God has not promised it will be easy. He has not put lots of concessions and rest stops on the escape route. There are hills to climb and obstacles to hurdle if we are to outwit and outrun the devil. The path of escape has but one entrance ramp and infinite exits. No one travels the path of escape by accident. For these reasons it is not a crowded path (Matthew 7:14). In fact, it can be lonely at times. But there is always at least one other who is faithful to show you the way.

EVE'S PUNISHMENT PRONOUNCED (GENESIS 3:15–16)

The most dismal part of the story of Eve comes as God pronounces His punishment on her. The purity and innocence of Eden is now history, and guilt has replaced the happiness of communion with God.

Thus, God pronounces for Eve sorrow in childbearing; for Adam, sweat and toil in providing food; and for both, death. They are then driven from Eden in the shadows of sin.

List and discuss three punishments of Eve.

_____

_____

Give reasons that reproductive issues such as premenstrual syndrome and post partum syndrome could be aspects of Eve's punishment?

_____

_____

God did not leave man without hope. In Genesis 3:15, a redeemer is promised—a remedy for sin. "And I will put enmity between you and the woman, and between your seed and her Seed; He shall bruise your head, and you shall bruise His heel" (Genesis 3:15).

The seed of woman is Christ (Galatians 3:16; 4:4). His heel would be bruised at Calvary. But Satan's head would be crushed as Christ overcame death. Thus, Christ would receive an injury, but would overcome in the resurrection. Satan would receive a fatal blow.

From this brief mention of the gospel, the scheme of redemption begins to unfold.

This shadow signals the beginning of the battle for the souls of humanity. The conflict rages through the Old Testament, climaxes at Calvary, ends at the empty tomb, and finds its eternal terms of peace in Acts 2.

How was Christ's heel bruised?

How was Satan's head crushed?

EVE'S FAMILY

It is at the birth of Eve's first son, Cain, that we may assume that God once again rules Eve's life. Her comment is: "I have acquired a man from the Lord" (Genesis 4:1).

She later bore Abel (Genesis 4:2), Seth (Genesis 4:25), and other sons and daughters (Genesis 5:4).

How does Psalm 127:3-5 relate to Eve's comment in Genesis 4:1? In what sense are parents stewards of souls?

In 1 John 2:15-17 we read that all that is in the world—all sin—can be categorized in at least one of three ways. Make a list of sins and place each one in one of the categories below.

Lust of the flesh	Lust of the eyes	pride

⤳ *Cindy's Reflections* ⤳

There Is a Way

He is there before you know it:
Lurking, waiting for a chance
To besiege you with his sparkle
In your unsuspecting glance.

He is solid. With his muscle
He can strike a deadly blow
To your strongest aspirations;
To the faith from which they grow.

You could never recognize him;
He is poised and quite well dressed.
In his confidence and kindness
He is reaching for your best.

He will back you in a corner
With his calm, seductive air.
Then you'll finally recognize him
As you cry out in despair.

Your cry, though penetrating,
May never reach a mortal ear;
But transcends up to the mind of God,
For He will always hear.

And He'll provide an answer,
Though it may be quite obscure
He has promised a deliverance
That His people may be pure.

God has promised in your darkness
He will guide you to the day.
So grasp the everlasting arm—Escape!
There is a way.

Chapter 2

The Beast within the Beauty
The Daughters of Men

Following Eve's introduction of sin into the newly created world, the true utopia of Eden was reduced to a brief moment in history. Within the span of only a few generations, sin became so pervasive that the wickedness of man was great in the earth, and God was grieved.

> The sons of God saw the daughters of men, that they were beautiful; and they took wives for themselves of all whom they chose . . . Then the Lord saw that the wickedness of man was great in the earth, and that every intent of the thoughts of his heart was only evil continually (Genesis 6:2–5).

"WIVES . . . WHOM THEY CHOSE"

The great flood of Genesis 7 is known to all Bible students as the only worldwide destruction in history. The reason for worldwide destruction was simple—worldwide sin. The reason for worldwide sin is found in Genesis 6:2—the "sons of God" married the "daughters of men." Thus, "the wickedness of man was great in the earth." The people of God lost their distinctiveness and became mingled with the ungodly. They even began to marry them because of their outward beauty, thus forgetting and defiling their purity as a separate people of God.

The first few verses of Genesis 6 set forth a powerful lesson for today's youth. Notice that the sons of God began to look upon the daughters of men indiscriminately. The only quality that they observed was that the daughters were beautiful. Whether they were daughters of God or daughters of men apparently made little difference. As Albert Barnes has aptly stated regarding this passage: "When God's children lose sight of such basic distinctions and look only for the pretty faces and shapely forms, then surely degeneracy has set in" (Leupold, H. C., D.D., Exposition of Genesis [Grand Rapids, MI: Baker Book House, 1942] p. 252.)

What practical characteristics should a Christian girl desire in a potential mate? Add to this list:
  Studies his Bible daily
  Leads prayer at the table when we go out to eat
  Respects elderly people

Why Marry a Christian?

What are the implications in this lesson for young people today? The obvious lesson that emerges is the importance of Christians marrying Christians. Notice these arguments in favor of marrying within the church.

❋ Your Christian mate will love you as Christ loved the church (Ephesians 5:25). Because of this unfailing love and because he shares your Christian values, he will respect you (Ephesians 5:23–33). He will practice the Golden Rule of daily living in your home (Matthew 7:12). You will occupy a position of honor in the marriage relationship (1 Peter 3:7).

Your Christian mate will share your supreme goal in life.

❋ Your Christian mate will share your supreme goal in life. This unity of purpose will be the basis of an ever-strengthening bond as you work together to achieve this goal (1 Peter 1:9).

> Comment on the difference between being a "member of the church" and being a "Christian." What is the literal meaning of the word Christian? How is this significant in looking for a mate?
>
> _____
>
> _____
>
> _____

Why Not Marry a Non-Christian?

Marriage counselors agree that religiously divided homes have certain built-in problems. No matter how we may tend to minimize religious differences, such basic values are ingrained within personalities. In a partnership such as marriage, it is of utmost importance to each partner to be able to share all phases of living. If religious beliefs are too diverse, couples will undoubtedly encounter problems.

Surveys have shown that in religiously divided homes conflict often occurs over church attendance or over which religion the children will be taught. Other frequently reported problems are interference by in-laws concerning religion and conflict over size of family and spacing of children.

> List and discuss other points of conflict that occur in spiritually divided marriages.
>
> _____
>
> _____

For the Christian, ultimate success in marriage can be found only in a relationship where both partners are working toward heaven. A recent survey in one congregation revealed that only six percent of its high school graduates who were divorced had divorced when both mates were Christians, while the remaining ninety-four percent of the divorces had occurred in religiously mixed marriages. While brotherhood-wide statistics, to my knowledge, have not recently been gathered, it has been my personal observation that while occasionally a Christian will successfully convert a non-Christian mate, this does not occur in the vast majority of cases. I have also observed that children pay a high and often eternal price while Mama tries to bring Daddy to the Lord. The survey referenced earlier tracked high school graduates' church attendance patterns. Of those young adults who no longer attend services, seventy-eight percent had religiously mixed marriages.

A business venture would be considered unsound if there were only a minimal chance of its success. Christians must consider the eternal risks of a marriage to a non-Christian.

The Christian woman must consider her own soul and guard it against unnecessary temptations. She is likely to jeopardize her eternal destiny in giving her life to, and becoming one flesh with, one whose influence will not lead her toward heaven (Matthew 6:33).

In choosing a companion for life, it is important to remember the fate of the world when the sons of God began to marry the daughters of men. How careful Christians must be to choose as close associates only those people who can bring out the best in them. After all, it is from this circle of friends that a lifetime companion will be chosen. What a precious relationship exists in marriage when two Christians love, work, and walk together in a cause bigger than life itself.

Several times I've been asked if I believe it is a sin for a Christian woman to marry a non-Christian. It has been my experience to note that women of deep conviction are not interested in dating or marrying men who are not disciples. Why would a woman who is diligently seeking first the kingdom—absorbing God's Word into her thoughts and lifestyle and constantly asking for His wisdom in her decisions—place herself in a position of submission to one who has never even become His child? I believe the frequent occurrence of such marriages is a direct result of worldliness before and during the dating years. If we dress, act, and party like the world at age fourteen, then becoming involved with and marrying someone of the world at age twenty is not a big leap.

Such marriage is a direct result of worldliness.

While 1 Peter 3:1 indicates that some women in the early church were married to non-Christians, and indeed could remain faithful in such a situation, it is my judgment that such women likely heard the gospel after they were married. I know women today who have become Christians after marriage. It is the responsibility of these women, so long as their marriages are scriptural unions, to live godly lives of submission in hopes of reaching their lost mates for the Lord. But it would be uncharacteristic of true Christianity to choose to enter a covenant so strong and sacred as marriage with one who does not obey the word (1 Peter 3:1).

Explain your belief about whether or not it is a sin for a Christian woman to marry a non-Christian man?

_____

_____

Are biblical principles of submission applicable when such a marriage occurs? Why or why not?

_____

_____

Cindy's Reflections

A Place of Harmony

Twenty years to teach them;
Twenty years to try;
Twenty years of prayer and praise . . .
Now they've learned to fly.

It's more than mere coincidence
That gathers us today.
It's toiling, tears, and tenderness
And hearts that learned to pray.

You remember yesterday . . .
The sweetness of a time
Of snaggletoothed smiles and blondish curls,
And innocence sublime.

But time marched on relentlessly
And memory took that day.
Now time holds out a new one
And in its dawn we pray.

To thank Him for the memories
And guidance from above;
And most of all, for His dear Son
To bless this bond of love.

This is a place of sweet goodbye.
We knew they couldn't stay;
And in our hearts we wouldn't
Have it any other way.

For it's a place of harmony.
The union that they share
Is everything we've dreamed for them . . .
The answer to our prayer.

Chapter 3

At All Cost

The Daughters-in-Law of Noah

Many times throughout life, we are faced with difficult decisions. Often we are forced to sacrifice things that mean a great deal to us for things that are even more important. Such is the case with the daughters-in-law of Noah.

There are many things that are not revealed about these three interesting characters of Genesis 7. We do not know their ages, anything about their families, or even their names. Even so, they become significant as we glean from them valuable lessons for our lives today.

Though Noah is the prominent character in the account of the great flood, in order to understand the sacrifices of his daughters-in-law, let us consider it from their point of view. Notice the things they sacrificed to remain faithful to God.

THEY SACRIFICED THEIR FAMILIES.

It is reasonable for us to assume that the families of these three women died in the flood. Unless they died prior to this account, they were somewhere in the mass of unbelievers thinking only of evil (Genesis 6:5) and refusing to hear Noah's call to repentance.

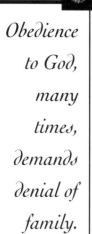

Obedience to God, many times, demands denial of family.

Thus we see three women in the midst of a scoffing multitude forsake their parents, likely realizing that from the safety of God's ark, they would watch them drown. This decision to maintain their faith in the God of the living was likely the most difficult one they were ever called upon to make.

Obedience to God, many times, demands the denial of family. In the case of Saul and Jonathan, we see a father attempting to smite his son with a spear as the son refuses to participate in the evil of his father (1 Samuel 20:30–34). How tragic it is when families are not united in service to God.

Yet, how much worse to see children sacrifice devotion to God and eternal life to pursue the sins of parents in a path that leads both parents and children to an eternal hell. The words in Matthew 10:34–38 are difficult to accept. Separation from family for any cause tears at the very substance of our lifestyle. But for Jesus, these words were not mere rhetoric. After all, His decision to be separated from His Father at Calvary had already been made.

> Do not think that I came to bring peace on earth. I did not come to bring peace but a sword. For I have come to "set a man against his father, a daughter against her mother, and a daughter-in-law against her mother-in-law"; and "a man's enemies will be those of his own household." He who loves father or mother more than Me is not worthy of Me. And he who loves son or daughter more than Me is not worthy of Me. And he who does not take his cross and follow after Me is not worthy of Me (Matthew 10:34–38).

How many times have you heard these or similar words? "I would become a Christian, but if I did, I would be condemning my deceased father [or mother or other relative] to hell."

The truth is that no one can condemn anyone else to hell. If one dies outside Christ, he is already condemned to hell. The only destiny that we can determine is that of our own souls. Though we cannot, by our own obedience, cause another to suffer in hell, we can by our own obedience avoid it for ourselves. No matter how hard it may be, truth must be thicker than blood. The only way for millions to be saved is by a rejection of their parents and families.

Give an example from your experience of someone who sacrificed close family relationships upon obeying Christ? How did this sacrifice make future faithfulness harder or easier?

THEY REJECTED THE RELIGIOUS TRADITIONS OF THEIR PAST.

We know little about the religion of the people of Noah's day, but we do know that most rejected the true God. In their acceptance of the God of Noah, these women put aside the traditions of their past. A tremendous faith is required to sever religious ties that have been woven throughout a lifetime.

Today we are handed a full menu of religious choices. Denominations and doctrines seem ever to multiply around us. The New Testament, however, is clear in its teaching regarding the oneness of the church. Notice these passages:

❄And I also say to you that you are Peter, and on this rock I will build My church, and the gates of Hades shall not prevail against it (Matthew 16:18).

❄But He answered and said, "Every plant which My heavenly Father has not planted will be uprooted" (Matthew 15:13).

❄Not everyone who says to Me, "Lord, Lord," shall enter the kingdom of heaven, but he who does the will of My Father in heaven. Many will say to Me in that day, "Lord, Lord, have we not prophesied in Your name, cast out demons in Your name, and done many wonders in Your name?" And then I will declare to them, "I never knew you; depart from Me, you who practice lawlessness!" (Matthew 7:21–23).

❄There is one body and one Spirit, just as you were called in one hope of your calling (Ephesians 4:4).

Are you a member of the one church, or will you be a part of the plant rooted up? Religions of men must be forsaken if we are to rest in the ark of salvation.

How does 1 Peter 3:20–21 call people to rest in God's ark of safety today?

_____

What act is necessary for salvation according to verse 21?

_____

THEY REJECTED THE MAJORITY.

The daughters-in-law of Noah likely heard friends and family scoff as they climbed aboard the big boat. Multitudes were convinced of the folly of Noah's warnings; they considered his preaching to be absurd. Perhaps religious leaders of the day even made speeches about the ridiculous flood scare. At any rate, their scoffing ended, as did their lives, in a horrible drowning.

It is interesting to notice the recurring downfall of the majority:

❄The majority died at Sodom and Gomorrah (Genesis 19).

❋The majority of Jacob's sons wanted to sell Joseph (Genesis 37).

❋The majority of the twelve spies lacked faith (Numbers 13).

❋The majority of the Israelites who left Egypt never entered the promised land (Numbers 14:23–24).

❋The majority killed Jesus (Matthew 27).

❋The majority will die in hell forever (Matthew 7:13–14).

It is easy to look about us and be drawn to go the way of the multitude. It is easy for young people to say, "Most of the kids at school cheat," or "Most of the kids will be at the ballgame tonight instead of at worship." The list could go on and on. Sometimes as we look about us, it is easy to wonder how so many could be wrong. But historically, the majority has always been wrong. "You shall not follow a crowd to do evil" (Exodus 23:2).

Historically, the majority has always been wrong.

What other biblical examples can you cite when the majority was wrong?

_____

Give examples of instances in which Christian women must forsake the majority today. Apply the separation that God requires to areas of living, such as entertainment choices, clothing, faithfulness to worship, and submission in the home.

_____

_____

_____

Though we know little of the daughters-in-law of Noah, we know they were determined to serve Jehovah at all cost. They evidently were not born into God-fearing homes. They rather learned to fear God through an association with His people. There was nothing that meant enough to them to interfere with their service to God. Is there anything that means that much to you?

Which of the three things cited that were forsaken by these women was likely most difficult and why?

Cindy's Reflections

Be a Light

Lend a hand. Take a stand. Guide a soul toward the goal.
In the fight, do what's right.
Be a light!

You've been blessed so share your best. Offer rest to one oppressed.
Bear a load on life's road.
Be a light!

Steady someone who is falling. Answer someone who is calling.
With open heart do your part.
Be a light!

Take a minute, praying in it. You'll be glad for how you spent it.
God will hear you and draw near you.
Be a light!

Share the Spirit through the Word. You've a friend who hasn't
heard. Stay aglow. Let her know.
Be a light!

Satan's power makes life dark. You could be some life's spark.
A shining ray, break of day.
Be a light!

Plant a seed. Pull a weed. Fill a need. Intercede.
One's depending on your befriending.
Be a light!

You can't heed all who need. You can't bandage all who bleed.
But think it through and answer true . . . is there just one who
looks to you?
Be a light!

CHAPTER 4

SEEKING FOR A CITY

SARAH

The most beautiful tribute to Sarah's virtuous life is found in Hebrews 11:11–16. She was truly a pilgrim in search of a country. Because of her faith, God has prepared for her a heavenly country.

THE VIRTUES OF SARAH

FAITH

Certainly the first positive quality of Sarah that comes to mind is her tremendous faith. Her character was such that, hundreds of years after her death, the writer of Hebrews included her in the list of great examples of faith. "By faith Sarah herself also received strength to conceive seed, and she bore a child when she was past the age, because she judged Him faithful who had promised" (Hebrews 11:11).

She was among those who did not receive the promises, but saw them afar off. She was one who confessed that she was a pilgrim on the earth (Hebrews 11:13). She sought for a country, a city prepared by God (Hebrews 11:16). How great must have been the faith of Sarah to have been mentioned in this list among such greats as Noah, Abraham, Joseph, and Moses!

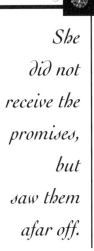

She did not receive the promises, but saw them afar off.

James 2:20 tells us that faith without works is dead. We must show our faith by our works (James 2:18). What then did Sarah do to show her faith as commended in Hebrews 11:11? Take a closer look. She "bore a child when she was past the age, *because she judged Him faithful who had promised* [emphasis added]." Here we see the birth of Isaac—the beginning of the Hebrew nation and the miraculous link in the lineage of Christ—a result of Sarah's great faith.

How many dynamic feats could we accomplish in God's service if we would only "judge Him faithful who has promised"! We certainly would forsake the world and be dedicated to the kingdom if we really believed in the promise of Matthew 6:31–33. Things that are so vitally important in our lives would pale in significance if we really thought that God would judge each of us personally. (Romans 2:16.) Our day might be altered considerably if we really realized that Christ could come today (Revelation 3:3). How many lives would be changed

In what areas do you find it difficult to "judge Him faithful"? Commit to daily prayer about these areas.

How would lives of lukewarm Christians today change if they "judged him faithful" as he promised in Matthew 6:33? Give practical scenarios.

if every sinner could see heaven or hell for just one second! But these things are not seen. "Faith is . . . the evidence of things not seen" (Hebrews 11:1). In this lifetime, faith is all we have of the unseen promises of God. Do we really judge Him faithful?

Because of Sarah's faith in God's promise, Isaac was born, Israel became a nation, and eventually Christ was born of her seed. Abraham is called the "father of the faithful," and those who obey Christ today are spiritual heirs or children of Abraham through faith (Galatians 3:29). In light of this, could we not fittingly style Sarah as the "mother of the faithful" and Christian women today as the "daughters of Sarah"? First Peter 3:6 verifies this.

SEPARATION

The first five verses of Genesis 12 find Abraham and Sarah being called out of their homeland to follow God into an unknown land. Together they accepted the challenge to leave friends, loved ones, and customs behind in the only land they had ever known. Hebrews 11:8 tells us that they did not even know the point of their destination. Again, a tremendous faith is displayed. It is not only God's requirement for trust in His promises that we see on this occasion, however. Here we also see another instance of God's eternal insistence that His people be separated (2 Corinthians 6:17–18), distinctive (Matthew 5:43–48), and special (peculiar KJV) (Titus 2:14).

What a temptation it must have been for Sarah to argue with God! She could have reasoned that her service to God could be rendered in her homeland more effectively than in a land of strangers. By her willingness to follow the Lord and leave the multitude, she became a key figure in God's scheme of redemption. Likewise, Christians today must leave the world behind and dare to be different. God often needs us most in a land of strangers.

> In what ways must Christian women today be societal non-conformists?
>
> _____
>
> _____

OBEDIENCE

The writer of Hebrews, as has already been cited, commends to us the great faith of Sarah. Peter commends to us her obedience to her husband: "As Sarah obeyed Abraham, calling him lord, whose daughters you are if you do good and are not afraid with any terror" (1 Peter 3:6).

Sarah recognized the supremacy of Abraham and gladly lived in subjection to him. In patriarchal times, wives often used the term lord in reference to their husbands. It signified a respect for them as rulers of the home. Although Christian women today are not required to use this term in addressing their husbands, they are required to show the honor that it denoted (1 Peter 3:1).

> Since submission in the home is not popular in our feministic society, suggest practical ways we can teach our daughters submission.
>
> _____
>
> _____

HOSPITALITY

"Do not forget to entertain strangers, for by so doing some have unwittingly entertained angels" (Hebrews 13:2).

Who unwittingly entertained angels? This passage could very well be a reference to Genesis 18. In this account, three men visited the tent of Abraham and Sarah. Abraham ran to greet them and together he and Sarah prepared a meal for them. One of these guests revealed His identity as the Lord Himself. Abraham and Sarah were not hesitant to show hospitality to these strangers. The visit proved to be quite eventful as, during the passage of it, Abraham and Sarah were promised a son and warned of the coming doom of Sodom and Gomorrah.

The writer of Hebrews points out an application of this lesson for us today. By extending hospitality to our fellowmen, we bring blessings to ourselves. Never should we forfeit the opportunity to entertain godly guests. Their presence and company often influence the home for eternal good. Our homes should always be open to ministering servants of the Lord.

Let us not forget that the admonition specifies hospitality to the stranger. This might include any lonely, hungry, needy, or lost person to whom we have the opportunity to extend hospitality (1 Peter 4:9; Romans 12:13). A husband might often be given to hospitality, but let us remember that a husband would have a difficult time entertaining guests without the cooperation of his wife. Much depends on the hospitality of the lady of the house.

By extending hospitality, we bring blessings to ourselves.

Why is our society moving away from hospitality? What can we do to encourage hospitality in the local congregation?

_____

_____

Have a class member bring hospitality tips to share with the class (Example: Tell how to arrange a welcoming guest room or how to encourage visitors to the services or even how to set a table properly).

_____

THE VICES OF SARAH

SHE HAD FALTERING FAITH.

One of the greatest proofs of the inspiration of the Bible is the fact that it reveals both the admirable and the evil aspects of its heroes and heroines. We see often, even in the champions of faith of Hebrews 11, a weaker side that falters in the face of temptation. Such is the case with Sarah. A study of her mistakes should serve to equip us against those same mistakes.

SHE ALLOWED BEAUTY TO INTERFERE
WITH HER SERVICE TO GOD.

In Genesis 12:11, 14, we learn that Sarah was fair to look upon. Beauty should be recognized as a blessing from God and should be used in His service. Sarah failed miserably and allowed her beauty to get her into more trouble than she could handle.

The scene is ancient Egypt. A caravan arrives on its outskirts. At the head of the caravan we see Abraham and his beautiful wife, Sarah. From their conversation we see that Abraham is afraid that the men of Egypt will be captivated by the beauty of Sarah and that they will murder him to get to her. Thus they devise a deceptive scheme:

> Therefore it will happen, when the Egyptians see you, that they will say, "This is his wife"; and they will kill me, but they will let you live. Please say you are my sister, that it may be well with me for your sake, and that I may live because of you (Genesis 12:12–13).

Sarah's beauty is about to put her into a position in which she can stand for truth and right. She can even persuade her husband to repent of his willingness to deceive. She will soon be in a position to be remembered as the woman who stood for truth, even against her husband. Sadly, she is going to do none of these things. She will fall to the temptation of her husband. She will agree to Abraham's plan. She is about to begin a new series of troubles.

The caravan reached Egypt. The Egyptian princes noticed the beauty of Sarah right away and commended her to Pharaoh. Abraham and Sarah executed their counterfeit, half-true scheme and told them that they were brother and sister. (Actually, Sarah was a half-sister to Abraham.) The king was impressed with Sarah and gave Abraham expensive gifts.

It was only when the Lord plagued Pharaoh's house that the king realized that he had been deceived. He quickly reprimanded them and sent them out of Egypt.

An ugly situation that marred the influence of Abraham and Sarah could have been avoided if Sarah had known how to handle her beauty as a blessing from God. How many times today do women misuse the physical beauty that God has given them? Consider these "Sarahs" of our modern day:

*The young lady who chooses to expose her shapely form rather than to follow God's command to dress modestly (1 Timothy 2:9). (Notice this command makes no exception for cheerleaders or athletes or even beauty queens. It does not indicate that it applies only in cold weather. It makes no exception for swim wear.)

*The young lady who allows a boyfriend to use her body to satisfy his lusts (Galatians 5:19).

*The young lady who allows her body to be used for evil purposes such as prostitution and pornography (Romans 12:1).

> *This command makes no exception for cheerleaders, athletes, or beauty queens.*

Find other examples of beautiful women in scripture. Did they use their beauty in service or did they allow it to be a snare?

_____

_____

SHE FAILED TO LEARN FROM HER MISTAKE.

After her shameful expulsion from Egypt, it would seem that Sarah would have learned her lesson. In Genesis 20 we find an episode, however, that proves to the contrary: "Now Abraham said of Sarah his wife, 'She is my sister.' And Abimelech king of Gerar sent and took Sarah" (Genesis 20:2). This time God revealed the truth to King Abimelech in a dream.

SHE ALLOWED HER FAITH TO WAVER.

In Genesis 12, God promised Abraham a great posterity. Obviously, for his seed to multiply, he must have a child. In Genesis 16, we find that the years had rolled on and Sarah was childless. She began to wonder just how God was going to bring about this great nation. Her faith began to waver, and she even decided to help God fulfill His promise:

> So Sarai said to Abram, "See now, the Lord has restrained me from bearing children. Please, go in to my maid; perhaps I shall obtain children by her." And Abram heeded the voice of Sarai (Genesis 16:2).

Again, her failure to trust the Lord proved to be a mistake that would only lead to more mistakes, one of which is found in the same chapter.

The handmaid of Sarah, at Sarah's request, gave birth to a son by Abraham. When Hagar conceived, she looked on Sarah with disdain, since Sarah was barren (Genesis 16:4). Sarah's response was an uncaring one. The Scriptures say she dealt harshly with Hagar (v. 6).

In Genesis 18:9–15, Sarah's lack of trust in the Lord is seen once again. Upon hearing the Lord's promise that she would bear a son, she reacted with levity. "Therefore Sarah laughed within herself, saying, 'After I have grown old, shall I have pleasure, my lord being old also?'" (Genesis 18:12). The Lord, detecting her lack of faith, responded, "Is anything too hard for the Lord? At the appointed time I will return to you, according to the time of life, and Sarah shall have a son" (Genesis 18:14).

Again, her doubt led to sin. In verse 15, she denied laughing. She lied! Even though later commended for her faith, she seemed to find it difficult to believe that nothing is too hard for the Lord.

Sarah, a colorful character, could be adequately described in many different ways:

beautiful	obedient	faithless
devoted	hospitable	harsh
faithful	deceitful	liar

Let us strive to exemplify her virtuous qualities and avoid the mistakes that caused her to falter.

Which attribute of Sarah would you most like to cultivate? Commit to pray daily concerning that attribute.

≈ Cindy's Reflections ≈

Make Your Home a Service Center

Today most Christian women in America are blessed with many luxuries within our homes. These blessings, while giving us a convenience of living that our great grandmothers never dreamed possible, also give us as stewards of God, untold opportunities to serve those around us. Ideas for serving from our homes are limitless and many are as old as Proverbs 31. Virtuous women have always reached out hands to the needy. As our resources increase, however, so do our opportunities.

Start in Your Kitchen

Your kitchen can become a center of service to others, beginning, of course, with your own family. It's always a good idea to make large dishes when you're cooking for your family, divide them before serving, and freeze one for a convenient standby when you have an opportunity to provide needed food for someone else. One lady I know operates an entire bread ministry from her kitchen. With her sourdough starter, she keeps multiple loaves of bread in her freezer, and constantly sends them, along with notes of encouragement to those who need a "picker upper." Another lady I know spends the summer canning juices and jellies and then uses them generously to stock the pantries of others through the year. The ideas are limitless. It's not as important what you do. Just be sure you're doing something with the opportunities that come your way. "She also rises while it is yet night, and provides food for her household, and a portion for her maidservants" (Proverbs 31:15).

Go to Your Dining Room

Hospitality is not only commanded of God's children; it is one of the most rewarding avenues of service for Christian women. The special privilege of having God's missionaries and preachers to share meals and their experiences of service in your home can be a tremendous source of strength for your family. Have neighborhood families over to share meals in hopes of sharing the bread of life with them, too. And don't forget families or individuals who are in need. Feeding a family whose breadwinner is sick or unemployed may be a small gesture on your part, but for them, it may truly be a blessing of physical and emotional nourishment. Remember, the food doesn't have to be fancy and the house doesn't have to be spotless. When we feed the hungry, we're feeding the Savior and he knows how to look beyond our houses into our hearts. "She extends her hand to the poor, yes, she reaches out her hands to the needy" (Proverbs 31:20).

Spend Time in Your Living Room

Our lives are so very busy that it's easy for us to limit our association with fellow Christians to the times when we assemble at the building. How tragic it is to miss the blessings that God's children experience as they share joys and sorrows, milestones and everyday occurrences, heart-to-heart conversations, laughter, and just chit-chat as a family, in the truest sense of the word. The family of God is your eternal family. The fellowship that God wants you to enjoy with fellow Christians, though immeasurably wonderful, has a great price tag. It will cost you time. The world around us leads us only to relationships that are convenient. God's children must often make time and occasions to grow close to those with whom they will share eternity. The burdens we can bear for each other are usually burdens of the heart. Until we truly know each other, our greatest needs are hidden. When Christians spend time with other Christians, then, avenues of fellowship and service and doors of opportunity become apparent. So take the time to develop your relationship as a sister. Go to the park, to the mall, or just to someone's shoulder and open up the living room in your life. You will find it is bigger than you thought. "On her tongue is the law of kindness" (Proverbs 31:26).

Find Quiet Moments in Your Bedroom

Perhaps we bear the burdens of those around us most effectively when we carry those burdens to our Father in prayer. Be sure to take time each day to search His Word for wisdom and then to approach Him specifically about the needs of those around you. Pray for your ministry—that is that you will, during this day, use the blessings He has given you to do the very most good possible for His cause. Some of the happiest people I know are people who spend all of their time confined to a bed or a chair, but who are able to meditate on God's Word and pray and minister to others through cards, calls, or just smiles. "A woman who fears the Lord, she shall be praised" (Proverbs 31:30).

Open Up Your Den

Most of us have casual friends who have never heard the gospel story. Although Satan gives us paranoia and all kinds of inhibitions about discussing our Savior with them, the fact that they are lost and that we are responsible for teaching them still remains. With the availability of video cassettes (such as the Jule Miller series) it is easier than ever to teach someone the gospel within the genial atmosphere of your own home. Despite the psychological hurdles that Satan throws in your path, you will find that most friends truly appreciate the interest you show in their spiritual well being. You will never regret sharing the truth. "She shall rejoice in time to come" (Proverbs 31:25).

Keep an Open Guestroom

Although you may not even have a guest room, you likely have someplace dry and warm where friends and family know that they are welcome. Make it available at every opportunity to your spiritual family, too. Remember the Shunammite woman who prepared a room for God's prophet? (2 Kings 4:1–37). Your life can be enriched, too, if you show hospitality to the people of God. Friends who are not Christians may want the peace and contentment of true Christianity if they experience it in extended visits in your home. "Let her own works praise her in the gates" (Proverbs 31:31).

Do You Have a Sewing Room?

I know one Christian lady who spent much of her fall during one particular year making lap quilts and teaching others to make them, too.

She saw that each patient in the nearby nursing home had one by winter. Another seamstress I know seems to be in constant demand for free mending and stitching for fellow Christians who may not have the equipment and expertise that she has. There are always children in nearby schools who are truly in need of clothing. Check with your school's guidance counselor. Remember, extra resources mean extra opportunities. "She seeks wool and flax, and willingly works with her hands" (Proverbs 31:13).

Use That Laundry Room

Look for those around you who may not be taking the convenience of washing and drying laundry at home for granted. A Christian family who is in the process of moving to your area may welcome the chance to come over and do laundry while they get to know you. Offer to launder the nursery and baptismal linens for your congregation or to wash the tablecloths after times of fellowship. Check on the family whose mother is ill or out of town. Throwing their laundry in with yours, though a small thing to you, will be a special blessing for them. "She . . . does not eat the bread of idleness" (Proverbs 31:27).

Do You Have a Home Office or Study?

One friend of mine who has a home computer has developed a unique way of service. She routinely makes colorful get-well banners using her computer and printer, brings them to services with her, puts them on the table in the foyer, and has an announcement made for all the members to write notes of encouragement on them and sign them. She then delivers them to patients at home or in the hospital to hang on the wall. They have been a smash hit with many who are ill or discouraged. They have graced many hospital, nursing home, and rehabilitation center walls as well as college dorm rooms for freshman who need encouragement from the home congregation. Other friends have developed wonderful scripture cards using their computers to send to ill or bereaving friends. You, too, can use your resources to respond to those around you who may be hurting. It only takes a moment to jot a scripture in a greeting card, but you may indelibly impress upon a hurting heart the fact that God's children, through His Word, have the answers to the problems of life. Grade correspondence courses, make bulletin boards, write a letter of encouragement to a new Christian or an unfaithful sister, a poem of thanks to someone who encouraged you. Use your talent and your resources, then add some initiative and reach out. "She reaches out her hands to the needy" (Proverbs 31:20).

Someone has said, "The blessings we receive in life are either windows through which we see God and other people, or they are mirrors through which we see only ourselves." Opportunity consists of someone's need and my ability to fill that need. "As we have opportunity, let us do good to all" (Galatians 6:10). Jim Elliott, a well-known missionary, said "He is no fool, who gives what he cannot keep, to gain what he cannot lose." Let's be sure that our investments are eternally secure. Let's use our resources, whatever they may be, to reach out and win souls, for when all other markets of this world have taken a final crash, investments in souls will have just begun to yield their highest dividends!

Chapter 5

A Portrait of Bondage

Hagar

One of the most confusing dilemmas of the religious world today is the problem of distinguishing between the old covenant and the new covenant. In the story of Hagar, an allegory is found that illustrates profoundly the inadequacy of the old law and the great promise of salvation found in the new law of Christ.

THE FACTS

Hagar was the Egyptian handmaid of Sarah. It is likely that she joined the caravan of Abraham and Sarah as it traveled through Egypt in their early wanderings. Most scholars believe that Hagar was a gift to Abraham and Sarah given by Pharaoh as a result of the deceit of Genesis 12. (See Genesis 12:10–16.)

Read Genesis 12:14–18. Hagar may have been a gift to Abram from Pharaoh (v.16) resulting from what sin?

List several complications brought about by Hagar's entrance into the lives of Abraham and Sarah.

The reader will recall that Sarah was quite aged, seventy-six to be precise, and had not been able to bear children. She remembered God's promise that a nation would come of Abraham's seed and, in her lack of faith, decided to help God. Her idea was to give her maid, Hagar, to Abraham. In this way, she reasoned, the heir of promise could be conceived by Hagar. (The practice of giving one's maid to one's husband was quite common in Sarah's day.) As is generally the case when faith begins to waver, Sarah's trouble had just begun, and this trouble was to affect deeply the life of Hagar.

What price did Hagar pay for Sarah's lack of faith?

THE SONS

Thus, Hagar's position suddenly changed from the handmaid of Sarah to the one who replaced her, at least temporarily, in the most intimate of all earthly relationships. The indication is that her attitude changed as quickly: "So he went in to Hagar, and she conceived. And when she saw that she had conceived, her mistress became despised in her eyes" (Genesis 16:4).

Sarah's reaction to Hagar's inflated pride was to complain to Abraham. He, in turn, told her to do with Hagar as she pleased. The Bible says that Sarah dealt harshly with her, and Hagar fled to the wilderness.

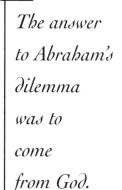

The answer to Abraham's dilemma was to come from God.

The next scene involving Hagar finds her beside a fountain of water in the wilderness. It was here that she received a visit from an angel who announced to her that she would have a son and that this son of Abraham would father a multitude. This son was later born and named Ishmael.

It was about fourteen years later that Sarah received her special visit from the Lord (Genesis 18). During this visit, of course, Isaac was promised. At the time of Isaac's birth, Ishmael was about fourteen years old. Perhaps his pride was smitten when he realized that Isaac, not he, would be the heir of promise. Ishmael made fun or mocked at the weaning festival of Isaac:

> So the child grew and was weaned. And Abraham made a great feast on the same day that Isaac was weaned. And Sarah saw the son of Hagar the Egyptian, whom she had borne to Abraham, scoffing (Genesis 21:8–9).

Sarah was displeased when she saw the son of Hagar mocking. She told Abraham to cast out Hagar and Ishmael. She refused to allow Ishmael to be heir with Isaac. Abraham, in a difficult position, was troubled. On one hand, his wife was insistent on casting out Hagar and Ishmael (Remember, Ishmael's very existence was Sarah's idea.) On the other hand, the mother of his son and even Ishmael, his son, were likely dependent on Abraham for their livelihood. The answer to his dilemma was to come from God:

But God said to Abraham, "Do not let it be displeasing in your sight because of the lad or because of your bondwoman. Whatever Sarah has said to you, listen to her voice; for in Isaac your seed shall be called" (Genesis 21:12).

Early one morning, Abraham placed bread and water on the shoulders of Hagar and sent mother and child away. Once again she went into the wilderness. When the water was gone, she put Ishmael under a shrub to die. She walked the length of a bow shot away from him so she could not see his death. She then lifted up her voice and wept.

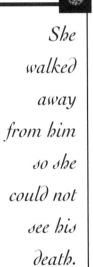

She walked away from him so she could not see his death.

Ishmael must have cried, too. The Bible says God heard his voice (Genesis 21:17). He calmed Hagar's fears promising to make of Ishmael a great nation. Then the Lord opened her eyes, and she saw a well of water.

From that day, God was with Ishmael. He grew and became an archer. The final account of Hagar in Genesis reveals that she chose Ishmael a wife out of the land of Egypt.

THE ALLEGORY

The concluding biblical record of Hagar is found in Galatians 4:21–31. (The King James Version refers to her in the New Testament as Agar.) It is here that the most significant lesson from Hagar may be learned.

One of the most important of all Bible lessons is the distinction between the law of Moses and the law of Christ. Without a knowledge of this distinction, it is impossible for one to know God's will for man today. A simple, yet powerful explanation of this lesson is found in this allegory concerning Sarah and Hagar. Hagar represents the law of Moses given at Mount Sinai. Sarah represents the law of Christ, or the second covenant. Let us compare the two covenants, using these two Bible women.

Hagar	Sarah
1. She was a bondmaid. (The law of Moses was temporary and could not loose the bond of sin.) (v. 22).	1. She was a free woman. (The law of Christ frees mankind from bondage.) (v. 22).
2. She had a son naturally or after the flesh. (The law of Moses offered no promise of salvation.) (v. 23).	2. She had a son miraculously or by promise. (The law of Christ offers a promise of salvation through the miraculous resurrection of Christ.) (v. 23).
3. She was in bondage with her son. (The old law could not give spiritual freedom and the Jews finally went into physical bondage.) (v. 25).	3. She was the mother of the child of promise. (Christians are children of the new covenant which offers a promise of salvation.) (vv. 26–28).
4. Her son persecuted Isaac. (The Jews persecuted Christians.) (v. 29).	4. Her son was mocked by Ishmael. (Christians were persecuted by the Jews.) (v. 29).
5. The bondwoman and her son were cast out. (The old law was cast out and the Jews were no longer God's chosen people.) (v. 30).	5. The son of the free woman was an heir. (The children of the new covenant are heirs of eternal life.) (v. 31).

How do some religious groups today fail to distinguish between the old and the new covenants?

_____

Which covenant offers salvation?

_____

Research: Which religious group today claims Ishmael as its father? What strife exists today between the modern country of Israel and this group?

❧ *Cindy's Reflections* ❧

Till Jesus

No offering for sin, no day at life's end. No victory to win
. . . till Jesus.

No light in the night, no strength for the fight, no plan for my
plight. . . till Jesus.

No redemption story, no Bethlehem glory, no empty grave, no
power to save,

No gospel for taking to all of the nations, no people of God for
sanctification,

No song for the angels, no purpose, no peace, no rest for the soul;
for its guilt, no release.

No Shepherd leading, no one interceding, no self sacrifice, no pearl
of great price,

No Savior slain, no blessing in pain, no heaven to gain
. . . till Jesus.

No crosses to bear, no comfort in prayer,

No crown to wear . . . till Jesus.

CHAPTER 6

FROM DELIVERANCE TO DESTRUCTION

WOMEN IN LOT'S FAMILY

LOT'S WIFE

The tragic story of Lot's wife is both begun and ended in fifteen words. These are found in Genesis 19:26: "But his wife looked back from behind him, and she became a pillar of salt."

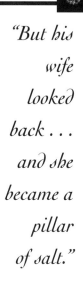

"But his wife looked back . . . and she became a pillar of salt."

The cities were doomed. The warnings had been issued. Lot's family had been hastily delivered from the mass destruction of Sodom and Gomorrah. Jehovah had been mindful of His people even in the midst of a wicked multitude. His instructions to them were both urgent and precise:

> So it came to pass, when they had brought them outside, that he said, "Escape for your life! Do not look behind you nor stay anywhere in the plain. Escape to the mountains, lest you be destroyed" (Genesis 19:17).

Sadly enough, in the midst of this great deliverance of the Lord, there was one who, having seen the salvation of the Lord, rejected the will and grace of God, and set her eyes once again on the cities. Her mistake and its fatal consequences are the subject of this lesson.

It might be noted here that there is some dispute among modern scholars as to whether Lot's wife became a literal pillar of salt in the same moment she sinned, or if she simply died instantaneously and the pillar of salt formed about her and became symbolic of her death. It is the belief of this writer that she instantly became a pillar of salt. Those who would discount the supernatural aspects of the event, or even proclaim it to be a myth, seem to forget the power of an almighty God and the faith that He demands.

THE LOOK OF DISOBEDIENCE

A mother once left a child alone with the following instructions: "Straighten your room and then go next door and play with Johnny until I return." Upon returning, the mother found the child next door playing with Johnny exactly as she had instructed. However, when the mother entered the child's room, she found that a part of her instructions had been ignored.

The point is obvious. The child had actually not obeyed at all. He had done precisely what he desired. Partial obedience is no better than disobedience. When one chooses which of the Lord's commands to heed, he is actually serving himself rather than the Lord. He has placed himself in the lawgiving position.

Lot's wife obeyed partially. God required her life for it. Two commands were given her. One was a positive command: "Escape for your life!" The other was a negative command: "Do not look behind you." She obeyed the first, but rejected the second. Her partial obedience indicates her love for what she had left behind. She chose to obey the first command, for it secured her very life. She disobeyed the second, revealing her self-centered passions. She, in truth, never obeyed at all. (Is this not the reason for the condemnation of the rich young ruler in Matthew 19:16–23?) Partial obedience is total disobedience.

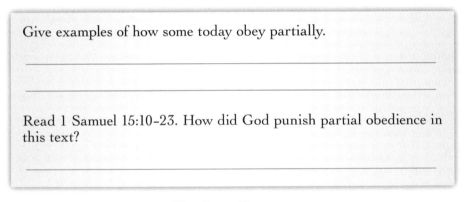

Give examples of how some today obey partially.

_____

_____

Read 1 Samuel 15:10–23. How did God punish partial obedience in this text?

_____

THE LOOK BACKWARD

Throughout the pages of the Word of God, a very sore punishment is pronounced on those who know and accept the Word of God, live according to His will, and turn again to sin. Our God expects us to appreciate the blessings of serving Him. We then, by experiencing these blessings and then choosing a life of sin, are in greater danger than if we had never obeyed at all. God's wrath upon those who look back is clearly demonstrated in Lot's wife's transition to a pillar of salt. She had received the salvation of the Lord. She had escaped the doom of Satan's domain. But she looked back.

Notice the following Scriptures regarding those who look back:

> And that servant who knew his master's will, and did not prepare himself or do according to his will, shall be beaten with many stripes.

But he who did not know, yet committed things deserving of stripes, shall be beaten with few. For everyone to whom much is given, from him much will be required; and to whom much has been committed, of him they will ask the more (Luke 12:47–48).

But Jesus said to him, "No one, having put his hand to the plow, and looking back, is fit for the kingdom of God" (Luke 9:62).

For if, after they have escaped the pollutions of the world through the knowledge of the Lord and Savior Jesus Christ, they are again entangled in them and overcome, the latter end is worse for them than the beginning. For it would have been better for them not to have known the way of righteousness, than having known it, to turn from the holy commandment delivered to them. But it has happened to them according to the true proverb: "A dog returns to his own vomit," and, "a sow, having washed, to her wallowing in the mire" (2 Peter 2:20–22).

The distinction between few and many stripes could not be clearer. The fact that those who look back are not fit for the kingdom of God pronounces certain doom on the Christian who turns again to the world. The scene of the dog returning to his vomit is a nauseating one. That is the attitude that God has—one of nauseating disgust for those who would forsake His mercy for the pleasures of sin.

Do we not, as Christians, have an even greater obligation than the alien sinner does? We know the truth. We can never return to the position of few stripes. We should soberly consider the consequences of looking back.

Find the proverb about the dog returning to his vomit in the Old Testament.

_____

THE LOOK THAT OUTLIVED HER

A single, sinful look was so abominable in the sight of Jehovah that it required the life of Lot's wife. It required the mother of two young daughters. It required the wife of a man who had just left his home and must now, alone, begin a new life.

Though the life of the sinner was extinguished and her body reduced to a motionless pillar of salt, the sin continued to live and multiply in her tragic memory. Recall the demoralizing sin of incest committed by Lot's daughters (Genesis 19). Would they have conceived children by their father if their mother had been by his side? Lot's sin of drunkenness and incest would probably have never occurred, and two idolatrous nations would never have existed had his wife been faithful to God.

Sin is always worse, in consequence, than the sinner expects it to be. One can hardly commit a sin only once. Sin is a snowballing proposition. The sin of Lot's wife lives yet in the memory of those who study God's Word. The brief and simple warning was stated by our Lord Himself: "Remember Lot's wife" (Luke 17:32)

LOT'S DAUGHTERS

In this brief but tragic account of unnamed women is found a succession of sinful deeds resulting in the birth of two wicked nations. The ruinous effects of sin are always greater than they seem in the face of temptation.

THE DESTRUCTION OF SODOM

The fearful destruction of Sodom and Gomorrah was at hand. The Lord had promised that if but ten righteous souls could be found within Sodom, the cities would be spared from the rain of fire and brimstone that was to fall upon them. Tragically, not even ten upright people of God could be found. Thus, in Genesis 19, Lot, the nephew of Abraham, and his family received a special visit from two angels of the Lord. After much insistence on Lot's part, the visitors entered his house to spend the night.

Sin's consequence is always worse than the sinner expects it to be.

The sin of homosexuality was apparently so prevalent at this time in Sodom, that groups of men wandered about seeking men who could be forced to fulfill the unnatural lusts that seemed to control their lives. (The Scriptures further address this sin in Romans 1:24–27.)

What is the meaning of sodomy?

_____

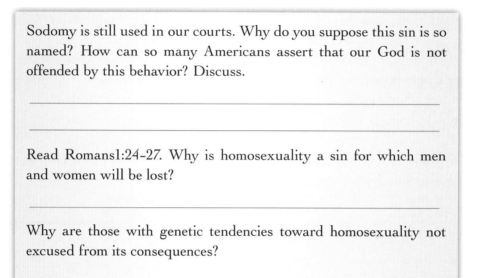

Sodomy is still used in our courts. Why do you suppose this sin is so named? How can so many Americans assert that our God is not offended by this behavior? Discuss.

_____

_____

Read Romans1:24-27. Why is homosexuality a sin for which men and women will be lost?

_____

Why are those with genetic tendencies toward homosexuality not excused from its consequences?

_____

In this case, men of all ages from "every quarter" circled the house and shouted their demands that Lot bring out the visitors that they might force their sinful sexual behavior on them. As they persisted, Lot's reply was a surprising one.

> See now, I have two daughters who have not known a man; please, let me bring them out to you, and you may do to them as you wish; only do nothing to these men, since this is the reason they have come under the shadow of my roof (Genesis 19:8).

Exactly why Lot offered these daughters to men of perversion is a matter of speculation. Perhaps he felt a deep responsibility to protect his guests, as visitors in Lot's day were given a position of extreme honor. Perhaps he knew that the men were actually angels. At any rate, he lacked faith in God's power to make a way of escape and attempted to substitute sin for sin. He offered to sacrifice the purity of his own daughters to avoid the sexual assault that seemed inevitable.

Why do you think Lot offered his daughters to these men?

_____

As God has always promised, He did provide the way of escape, and this first-recorded episode in the lives of Lot's daughters ended with

God's intervention. The men were determined to fulfill their lusts. They seemingly were not interested in the daughters but were ready to break down the door to reach the visitors. The angels opened the door and pulled Lot inside and smote the men outside with blindness "so that they became weary trying to find the door."

This is the environment to which Lot's daughters were accustomed. Imagine the temptations they must have faced every day! With every temptation, however, the Lord provides the way of escape (1 Corinthians 10:13). In this case, that way of escape was clearly routed for them.

During that same evening, the angels instructed Lot to gather his family and flee from Sodom. They warned that the city would be destroyed for "the outcry against them has grown great before the face of the Lord" (Genesis 19:13). The following morning the angels hastened Lot. They urged him to flee before the great destruction. Lot still lingered, and the Scripture says the men "took hold" of the hands of Lot, his wife, and two daughters and set them outside the city. Thus, the Lord delivered Lot's family out of temptations. (Read 2 Peter 2:7–9.)

> *The way of escape was clearly routed for them.*

Remains of Sodom

After the untimely death of their mother, we next see the daughters of Lot living in the caves with their father outside the city of Zoar. It seems that after the terrible destruction of their friends in Sodom that they would have abhorred evil (Romans 12:9). But such was sadly not the case. Though Sodom was destroyed, its influence lived on in the lives of the two women. They, too, perverted themselves sexually and committed incest. Association with those who are evil inevitably brings corruption. "Evil companionships corrupt good morals" (1 Corinthians 15:33 ASV).

Discuss the problem of rationalization of sin.

Give examples of other Bible characters who had a "good reason" to sin.

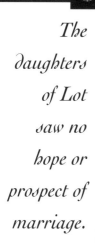

The daughters of Lot saw no hope or prospect of marriage.

The daughters of Lot, having been removed from their former companions, saw no hope or prospect of marriage. In their lack of faith in God and His power to provide, they began to rationalize. They reasoned that they should preserve seed of their father. Thus, they committed the sin of incest. Could we not, within our minds, excuse any sin if we were determined to commit it?

The plan was thus devised. They would first make Lot drink wine. Then they would lie with him in hopes of conceiving. On consecutive nights they carried out the plan. On the first night the older sister conceived, and on the following night the younger conceived. Their sons were named Moab and Ben-Ammi, respectively.

To what extent did the use of alcohol dull the moral senses?

_____

Discuss alcohol and date rape. (Have someone research the correlation.)

_____

Once again, as is always the case, their lack of faith bred moral corruption. Moab fathered a nation, the Moabites. It was Eglon, king of the Moabites, who oppressed the people of God in Judges 3:12–30. The Ammonites, children of Ben-Ammi, assisted him.

The Ammonites had many other clashes with the Israelites as well. (See Judges 11:4–33; 2 Samuel 10:6–14; 12:26–31.) They even became an obstacle in the rebuilding of the Jerusalem wall (Nehemiah 4:3–7). It seems that there is no such thing as a single sin.

CONCLUSION

Although the events of the lives of Lot's daughters are confined to one chapter of the book of Genesis, many truths for application in our lives can be gleaned from them:

❋No one is ever forced to sin. God will consistently provide the way of escape.

❋It is our responsibility to take advantage of the provided way of escape. It likely will not be the easiest or most desirable route, from a human standpoint.

❋The Scriptures are very plain in their condemnation of the sin of homosexuality.

❋We can never outlive the evil influences of ungodly associates.

❋We can rationalize or find a good excuse to commit any sin.

❋The use of alcohol is sinful and dulls the moral sense. Thus a person under its influence may commit sins that he would otherwise consider abominable.

❋An unchecked lack of faith always brings further corruption.

⇜ *Cindy's Reflections* ⇝

It's a Jungle Out There

Be ready. Be watchful. Be prayerful. Beware!
Be always on guard. Be careful! He's there.
He stalks like a lion, his prey to ensnare.
He's the king of the darkness in his jungle out there.

If he made a loud roar, you would know he's around.
But he creeps up behind, without making a sound.
Then with cords of worldly wisdom that seem so profound
He entraps you while you're sleeping. You don't even know you're bound.

That's the saddest thing about those cords that hold you in his power.
You're doomed and you don't realize the lateness of the hour.
You've grown to love his jungle. To his plans your will has cowered.
You don't know that you're the prey and in the end you'll be devoured!

So you learn the jungle lingo and you dance the jungle dance.
You swing like Tarzan, dress like Jane, and when you get the chance
You spread the jungle borders, binding others who were free,
And everything the lion wills is what you want to be.

Are you happy in the jungle? You would always answer "Yes.
I am doing what I love to do. This free life is the best!"
But your jungle is a doomed domain and with your king you're damned.
For the lion's long been conquered by the meek and mighty Lamb.

CHAPTER 7

THE BRIDE ADORNED

REBEKAH

THE STORY

No other woman in this study had greater opportunities for happiness and blessing than did Rebekah. We are all, however, the masters of our own lives. Opportunities are only entranceways. Often upon entering we find the pathway difficult and toilsome, albeit rewarding. Rebekah allowed her opportunity for great happiness to become marred by her lack of faith and by deception.

OPPORTUNITIES OFFERED

In a remarkable setting of romance, Rebekah is introduced. Our first picture of her portrays her with a pitcher on her shoulder approaching the well to draw water, perhaps for a meal at her father Bethuel's house. The Scriptures describe her as a very beautiful young woman, a virgin (Genesis 24:16).

Abraham's servant, sworn to find Isaac a bride from the homeland, at once ran to meet the beautiful girl, asking her for a drink. She politely complied. When the servant had finished drinking, she courteously drew water for the stranger's camels also. Little did she know that in this simple act of kindness she revealed herself to be the maiden for which the servant searched. Notice the sign for which the servant had asked the Lord in helping him to find the chosen maiden:

Her happiness was marred by lack of faith and deception.

> O Lord God of my master Abraham, please give me success this day, and show kindness to my master Abraham. Behold, here I stand by the well of water, and the daughters of the men of the city are coming out to draw water. Now let it be that the young woman to whom I say, "Please let down your pitcher that I may drink," and she says, "Drink, and I will also give your camels a drink"—let her be the one You have appointed for Your servant Isaac. And by this I will know that You have shown kindness to my master (Genesis 24:12–14).

Such a small opportunity to show concern for a fellow man became the open door for the richest of God's blessings upon Rebekah. So many times today we deny ourselves the blessings that are within our grasp by failing to take advantage of the God-given opportunities to do good. How many more people would hear the gospel each day if we took advantage of every opportunity to tell it? How much greater would our attendance be if everyone who had the opportunity to attend were present? How much less suffering and hunger would be experienced by the unfortunate if those whom God has richly blessed would avail themselves of the opportunity to help? Even more personally, how much stronger would you be if you grasped every opportunity to study, pray, and serve?

Opportunity is always on the move. It never stops to wait. One must grasp it as it comes or it is gone forever. Thomas Percy once wisely said, "He that would not when he might shall not when he would." Let us consider what inspiration says of opportunity and be prepared when it knocks on our door. "Therefore, to him who knows to do good and does not do it, to him it is sin" (James 4:17). "Therefore, as we have opportunity, let us do good to all, especially to those who are of the household of faith" (Galatians 6:10).

Why is it difficult to serve in small ways today?

_____

Have a class member research the events surrounding 1 Kings 20:40. What happened while someone was "busy here and there"?

_____

THE PARTIAL PARENT

Rebekah, with the decisiveness that always characterized her, chose to follow the servant to wed Isaac. Thus their lives together began with much happiness. "Then Isaac brought her into his mother Sarah's tent; and he took Rebekah and she became his wife, and he loved her. So Isaac was comforted after his mother's death" (Genesis 24:67).

The next chapter in Rebekah's life begins with a plea to God. She was childless. Her husband Isaac prayed that she might conceive. The Lord blessed her with not one child, but two. Rebekah was to be the mother of twins. When she felt a jostling within her womb and asked the Lord what this struggling meant, His reply was: "Two nations are in your womb, two peoples shall be separated from your body; one people shall be stronger than the other, and the older shall serve the younger" (Genesis 25:23).

The message was clear. Rebekah was to bear twins. Each twin would father a nation. Contrary to the tradition of the day which honored the oldest son with the blessings of wealth and power, in this case, the younger was to be blessed and to be the dominant of the two.

When the time of delivery came, the first to be born was a red, hairy boy. They named him Esau. He was followed by Jacob who was born holding the heel of Esau.

Thus, two sons were born. Two nations were begun. Esau grew to be a "man of the field" and "a skillful hunter." Jacob was rather a typical nomad, "a mild man, dwelling in tents" (Genesis 25:27). The children were obviously of two very differing characters.

The Scriptures then reveal a flaw in the character of Rebekah that resulted in great sorrow and sin in her later years. The Scriptures tell us that she was partial as a parent. "And Isaac loved Esau because he ate of his game, but Rebekah loved Jacob" (Genesis 25:28).

Partiality in a parent-child relationship is never good. Problems always result. The case of Isaac and Rebekah is no exception. Rebekah's partiality became her stumbling block. It caused her faith in God's promise of Jacob's supremacy to waver. She, like some of her predecessors, decided to devise her own plan to help God in the advancement of her favorite son, Jacob.

Discuss problems in families today due to partial parents, particularly the challenges of step-families.

_____

_____

List some practical do's and don'ts for moms in preventing any perceived favoritism. (Example: Don't let your children hear you comparing their qualities or achievements.)

_____

_____

THE DECEPTIVE WIFE

The years rolled on. Isaac grew old and began to prepare for his death. He called Esau, his older and favorite son, and instructed him to prepare venison, bring it before him, and receive the blessing. This blessing, of course, entailed the wealth, honor, and power that were generally granted to the firstborn.

Rebekah, however, had other plans. She quickly devised a deceptive scheme. (Note here that the lives of Isaac and Rebekah had been plagued by deceit on another occasion. A reading of Genesis 26:7–11 reminds us that Isaac perpetuated the sin of his parents in claiming that his wife was his sister. [See Genesis 12:13; 20:2.] Perhaps this deceit on Isaac's part played a part in the degradation of Rebekah's character.)

Rebekah forgot that God had a plan; she invented her own.

At any rate, Rebekah forgot that God had a plan for Jacob and thus invented the following one of her own. (Remember, a lack of faith always breeds sin.)

Jacob was to bring in goat meat for his mother to prepare for Isaac. Jacob was then to take it in to his nearly blind father and pretend to be Esau. In this way, Rebekah reasoned, he could receive the blessing that Isaac intended to place upon Esau. When Jacob objected, saying that his smooth skin would reveal his identity (Esau was a hairy man), Rebekah's determination to deceive is revealed in her reply: "Let your curse be on me, my son; only obey my voice, and go, get them for me" (Genesis 27:13).

Jacob got the meat and Rebekah prepared it. She put kidskins on the smooth skin of Jacob and sent him in unto his father.

Rebekah's scheme worked. Jacob was pronounced lord over his brother and heir of the wealth of his father, Isaac. Esau shortly came, expecting to be blessed, only to hear these words of his father: "Your brother came with deceit and has taken away your blessing" (Genesis 27:35).

Rebekah's partiality toward Jacob combined with her lack of faith in God's promise had prompted her to deceive the one for whom she had once given her all.

Why is it important that complete honesty exists between marriage partners?

_____

Can dishonesty in the home exist without negatively affecting the children? Discuss.

_____

_____

Can dishonesty in the home exist without negatively affecting the children? Discuss.

_____

_____

THE MISERABLE FAMILY

It was done. She planned and schemed to see it happen—and it did! Jacob had received the blessing according to Rebekah's plan, not the Lord's.

Which son, Jacob or Esau, was appointed by God to receive the blessing?

_____

List the sorrows encountered by Rebekah as a result of her failure to wait on the Lord.

_____

How has the era of fast food and "Wal-Mart convenience" made it ever more difficult for us to accept God's timetable?

_____

It seems that, having successfully deceived Isaac, Rebekah would have been happy. But sin never brings the contentment that it promises. Rebekah ruined her own life and the lives of those who meant the most to her.

✻*She disappointed Isaac.* She caused him to tremble when he learned of her deception (Genesis 27:33). She drove both of his sons away from him (Genesis 28:5, 9).

✻*She cruelly injured the life of Esau.* Because of her cruel injustice toward him, Esau willfully rejected his father's will and married foreign wives. These wives produced nations that became enemies of God's people (Genesis 28:8–9). He was also angered to the point of murder (Genesis 27:41).

She was forced to send her beloved Jacob away.

✻*She drove Jacob from home.* The object of her partiality, the one she attempted to promote, is perhaps the one she hurt the most. Her dear son was forced to run from Esau's wrath. He literally had to run for his life: "Arise, flee to . . . Haran . . . until your brother's anger turns away from you" (Genesis 27:43–45).

✻*She ruined the remnant of her own life.* Rebekah no longer had a trusting relationship with her husband. Her firstborn was filled with resentment and hate. She was forced to send her beloved Jacob away from her. The last chapter in the life of Rebekah closes with these tragic words: "What good will my life be to me?" (Genesis 27:46).

"Do not be deceived, God is not mocked; for whatever a man sows, that he will also reap" (Galatians 6:7).

THE ALLEGORY

Several times in the New Testament writings Christ is symbolized by the bridegroom, and the church is described as His bride (Revelation 21:2; Matthew 9:15; Mark 2:19; Luke 5:34; Matthew 25:1; John 3:28–29). May our appreciation for this church grow deeper as we consider its beauty as the bride of Christ.

ISAAC AND CHRIST

As a preface, notice several ways in which Isaac may represent our Savior:

✳*His supernatural birth* (Genesis 18:9–12; Luke 1:30–35).

✳*His virtuous life* (Genesis 22:6; Luke 2:49). (Both Isaac and Christ were about the business of their fathers.)

Abraham issued specific characteristics that the bride must have.

✳*His vicarious death.* (Vicarious means "done or suffered for others.") Isaac was actually offered in the mind of Abraham as Christ was offered to bear the sins of many (cf. Hebrews 11:17; Hebrews 9:28). Interestingly, both Isaac and Christ carried the wood to the site of the sacrifice (Genesis 22:6, John 19:17).

✳*His victorious resurrection.* God was able to raise up Isaac and Christ (cf. Hebrews 11:19 and Romans 8:34). Isaac was "raised" three days after he was offered in the mind of Abraham (Genesis 22:4). Christ arose on the third day (Luke 18:33; Acts 10:40).

All of these events in the life of Isaac occurred prior to the entrance of Rebekah into his life. They likewise preceded the establishment of Christ's church.

REBEKAH AND THE LORD'S CHURCH

Since prearranged marriages were customary in that day, Abraham sent a servant to seek a bride for Isaac (Genesis 24:1–4). Today, through His inspired Word, God seeks a bride for His Son Jesus (2 Corinthians 11:2; Revelation 21:2).

In Genesis 24:3–4, 8 we see that Abraham issued specific characteristics that the bride must have. She was not to be a Canaanite. She was to be of Abraham's kindred. Finally, she must be willing.

God also has set forth certain requirements through His Word for those who would be a part of the bride of Christ. To be eligible to be married to Christ, one must hear the gospel (Romans 10:17), believe that gospel (Mark 16:16), repent of sins (Luke 13:3), confess Christ (Romans 10:10), and be baptized for the remission of sins (Acts 2:38). These requirements must be met by prospective Christians just as Abraham's were met by Rebekah.

In comparing Rebekah to the bride of Christ, what could the servant represent?

_____

Who might Abraham represent?

_____

The servant, having noted the qualifications, had one last question before departing on his journey. This is recorded in Genesis 24:5: "Perhaps the woman will not be willing to follow me to this land. Must I take your son back to the land from which you came?" Notice carefully Abraham's reply: "And if the woman is not willing to follow you, then you will be released from this oath; only do not take my son back there" (Genesis 24:8).

Should the chosen woman be unwilling to come to Isaac, there would be no further attempt to unite her with him. The servant was no longer bound to find a bride.

OFFERED ONCE

How does this apply to us today? The comparison is simple. As the servant presented his offer to Rebekah, so the Bible today presents Christ's offering for sins to us: "So Christ was offered once to bear the sins of many. To those who eagerly wait for Him He will appear a second time, apart from sin, for salvation" (Hebrews 9:28). It is up to us, however, to accept or reject the sacrifice. No one will ever be saved against his will. "And the Spirit and the bride say, 'Come!' And let him who hears say, 'Come!' And let him who thirsts come. Whoever desires, let him take the water of life freely" (Revelation 22:17). If we choose to reject the invitation, no further provision will be made for us: "Nor is there salvation in any other, for there is no other name under heaven given among men by which we must be saved" (Acts 4:12). Our choice must be made. Will we accept the invitation and receive the blessings of

God as did Rebekah, or reject the bridegroom and forfeit the salvation He offers?

Upon reaching the homeland, the servant's task was not an easy one. After finding the ideal wife for Isaac, he was faced with the problem of convincing her to travel to a faraway land and marry a stranger, sight unseen. The servant described the wealth and blessings of God that Rebekah would inherit in her marriage to Isaac. Rebekah knew that this proposal meant that she must give up everything—her home, her family, and her friends. Yet, her answer was decisive: "Then they called Rebekah and said to her, 'Will you go with this man?' And she said, 'I will go'" (Genesis 24:58).

Jehovah today invites us to blessings and eternal wealth as the bride of Christ. To inherit these blessings, however, we must be willing to sacrifice all and follow Christ (Matthew 16:24). We cannot see Christ or heaven before we make our decisions, but by faith we must, like Rebekah, love Him and surrender ourselves to Him (1 Peter 1:8).

Will we reject the bridegroom and forfeit the salvation he offers?

READY FOR THE BRIDEGROOM

Finally, Rebekah may be compared to the church in that she made herself ready for the bridegroom and anxiously looked for him (Genesis 24:64–65). Christ the bridegroom is coming again. We, as His bride, must be prepared. We must be looking for Him. "Therefore you also be ready, for the Son of Man is coming at an hour you do not expect" (Luke 12:40). "So Christ was offered once to bear the sins of many. To those who eagerly wait for Him He will appear a second time, apart from sin, for salvation" (Hebrews 9:28).

In Matthew 25:1–13 we read the tragic parable of five foolish virgins who failed to prepare and watch for the bridegroom. This account closes with a warning that should cause each of us to consider soberly our answer to the bridegroom's invitation: "Watch therefore, for you know neither the day nor the hour in which the Son of Man is coming" (Matthew 25:13).

How beautiful is the story of Rebekah's union with her beloved Isaac! How meaningful it becomes when compared with the marriage of Christ and His church!

Note some comparisons between Rebekah and the church:

Rebekah	The Church
Rebekah was sought by a servant to be the bride of Abraham's son.	The church is sought by the Word to be the bride of God's Son.
Specific requirements were to be met by the bride.	Specific requirements are to be met by members of the church.
If she were unwilling to come, no further attempt would be made.	If one is unwilling to obey God, no further provision will be made.
Rebekah gave up her all to go to a husband and a home that she had not seen.	A Christian must deny self and follow a Savior to a home she has not seen.
Rebekah was ready and watching for Isaac.	The church must be ready and watching for Christ.

✑ *Cindy's Reflections* ✑

Sounds of God

A basketball bouncing on my drive;
A soft little song from a girl of five;
The buzz of bees, a whistling breeze;
The splash of the shower, the crash of a tower.

Disposal trashing, compactor smashing;
Clocks dinging, doorbell ringing;
Rain falling, children calling;
Vacuum roaring, someone snoring.

CNN bringing the voice of our nation
While Mama is chatting in phone conversation;
A guitar strumming, a dryer humming;
A microwave zapping, a Collie pup yapping.

Piano scales practiced on old worn-out keys;
Fireside conversations of old memories;
The squeaking of rockers on tired rocking chairs;
The patter of feet going up and down stairs.

The laughter at dinner, the jokes of a child;
The living room wrestling when everyone's wild;
The squibbles and squabbles of small girls and boys;
My! How God blessed us with all of this noise!

A father is telling the story of old;
A hymn in the night when the story is told;
The children petition their Father in prayer;
Sweet sounds of our home, for He lives with us there.

Do you ever take time at your house to be still?
And listen with ears that are turned to His will?
To sounds of His blessings . . . to voices that pray?
Does God live at your house? Have you heard him today?

CHAPTER 8

DIVIDED ALLEGIANCE

RACHEL

Rachel is remembered because she "built the house of Israel" (Ruth 4:11). Let us notice several other things for which she may be remembered and glean from her life those timeless truths that may enrich our own.

RACHEL IN ROMANCE

Following Jacob's deception of his aged father Isaac, the Scriptures follow Jacob to the homeland where his new life begins with the meeting of Rachel. His purpose for traveling to the homeland, Padan Aram, was twofold. First, he hoped to escape his brother Esau's wrath (Genesis 27:43–45). Second, he was to find a wife of his kindred (Genesis 28:1–2). He immediately began the accomplishment of the latter.

Upon arriving in Padan Aram, Jacob inquired of his father's kindred. He was informed that his cousin Rachel was approaching with the sheep. There, in a natural setting of romance similar to the one in which Rebekah had drawn water for the camels years ago in a nearby spot, Jacob watered the sheep of Rachel's father, Laban. If there has ever been a "love at first sight," this must have been it; for Jacob, even at this first meeting, kissed Rachel and wept (Genesis 29:11). He then wasted no time in asking Laban for her hand in marriage. Jacob had found his beautiful beloved bride.

RACHEL IN BIGAMY

How many problems could have been avoided in this beautiful union had deception not once again ruined an otherwise harmonious marriage. Just as deception marred the lives of Isaac's family, so it was to haunt Jacob throughout life.

For about a month after his arrival, Jacob lived with and worked for Laban, his uncle. After this first month had passed, he and Laban sat down at the bargaining table. Laban asked Jacob what he desired as wages for his work. Jacob replied without hesitancy: "I will serve you seven years for Rachel your younger daughter" (Genesis 29:18).

The intensity of Jacob's love for Rachel is unquestionable. The Bible says that his love for her made seven years (2555 days) seem as but a few days (Genesis 29:20).

After the seven years elapsed, a wedding feast was prepared. As was customary, Jacob's bride was likely escorted to him in silence and darkness. Jacob awoke the following morning only to find that he had married, not his beloved Rachel, but her less-favored, less-beautiful sister Leah. Laban had deceived the great deceiver.

After a week of marriage to Leah, Jacob was also given Rachel, but was required to work seven more years for her. Thus, deception had bred for Rachel a bigamous marriage and the beginning of a life of contention and rivalry.

It is perhaps difficult for the American woman today to comprehend the built-in problems of polygamy. God was aware of these when He, in His infinite wisdom, prescribed for marriage one man and one woman. "Therefore a man shall leave his father and mother and be joined to his wife, and they shall become one flesh" (Genesis 2:24).

Notice several problems that Rachel encountered in this three-way relationship.

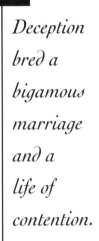

She was barren. The Scriptures tell us in Genesis 29:30 that Jacob loved Rachel more than Leah. In verse 31 we are told that when the Lord saw his favoritism, He opened Leah's womb, but Rachel was barren. It would appear that God sought to comfort Leah, the less-loved wife, by giving children to her, while perhaps teaching Jacob and Rachel to depend on His mercy rather than a physical attraction. At any rate, Rachel was seemingly miserable in her barren state.

She became envious. Envy may be defined as "discontent or ill will at another's good fortune because one wishes it had been his." It has plagued humanity since the time of Cain and Abel. Proverbs 14:30 describes it as "rottenness to the bones." In this case, Rachel was envious of Leah's fruitfulness in child bearing. "Now when Rachel saw that she bore Jacob no children, Rachel envied her sister, and said to Jacob, 'Give me children, or else I die!'" (Genesis 30:1). Envy led to further complications in Rachel's life. It is still a damning sin (Galatians 5:21).

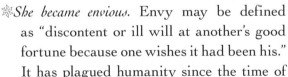

Deception bred a bigamous marriage and a life of contention.

List New Testament scriptures about the sin of jealousy ("envy" KJV). Discuss its materialistic effect on our society at large.

_____

_____

_____

To what sins is jealousy compared in Proverbs 27:4?

_____

✻*She lacked trust in God.* Barrenness was not a problem in the family of Abraham. Like Sarah, Rachel had lost faith in God's power to bless. Like Sarah, she ignored God's divinely instituted order of marriage by giving her husband a handmaid. And finally, like Sarah, she resorted to human invention rather than depending on God. She asked Jacob to "go in" to her handmaid, Bilhah, so she could "have children by her" (Genesis 30:3).

Sadly enough, Rachel viewed the child of Bilhah as a victory over Leah. She named him Dan, meaning "judge" or "vindication." Bilhah also bare another son, Naphtali, meaning "wrestling."

What lessons can women who have difficulty bearing children learn from this trial?

_____

RACHEL IN MOTHERHOOD

Just as had been the case with Sarah, God later proved His mercy to Rachel in the birth of a son, Joseph. It seems that, in the birth of Joseph, she finally recognized the power of God in relation to her own selfish efforts. She attributed her success in child bearing to God rather than to herself and trusted Him to give her even another son. "And she conceived and bore a son, and said, 'God has taken away my reproach.'

So she called his name Joseph, and said, 'The Lord shall add to me another son'" (Genesis 30:23–24).

RACHEL IN IDOLATRY

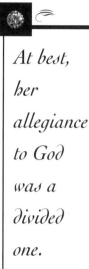

Thus the years rolled by in Rachel's contentious home. By and by, Jacob her husband became wealthy: "Thus the man became exceedingly prosperous, and had large flocks, female and male servants, and camels and donkeys" (Genesis 30:43).

Envy once again entered the family. This time Laban's sons, Rachel's brothers, became envious of Jacob's wealth. Thus, God told Jacob to return to the land of his childhood.

In the midst of all the packing and planning for the trip, Rachel stole the household gods—teraphim—from her father's house.

At best, her allegiance to God was a divided one.

The question of why she wanted to carry these idols with her is of some import. Perhaps she wanted to deprive her father of the blessings that she thought they could grant him. Perhaps she took them in hopes that she herself would receive good fortune by possessing them. Remember, she had come from a background of idolatry. The fact that she left her homeland in obedience to Jacob's God shows a measure of faith in Jehovah. But, at best, her allegiance to God was a divided one.

Anything that takes any part of the allegiance that rightfully belongs to God may be considered an idol. Are you involved in idolatry even today? Is your allegiance to God, at best, a divided one? One does not necessarily have to bow before a graven image to be idolatrous.

Laban never found the stolen images. He did pursue the caravan of Jacob and search for them. Rachel had hidden them in the camel's saddle. Notice the excuse she deceptively used for not arising from the camel's saddle: "'Let it not displease my lord that I cannot rise before you, for the manner of women is with me.' And he searched but did not find the household idols" (Genesis 31:35). (The "manner of women" is generally recognized as menstruation.)

Rachel indeed was given to idolatry. She proved her devotion to these inanimate objects by her willingness both to steal and deceive for them.

Why do we sometimes try to hide our idols today?

_____

_____

Our secret idols follow us just as Rachel's followed her from her father's house. Give examples of "secret idols" and explain.

_____

_____

Where do our secret sins follow us? (1 Timothy 5:24)

_____

_____

In Genesis 35:1-4, we find Jacob purging his household from idols. Rachel's stolen gods seemingly had multiplied. Discuss how a mother's idols today might "multiply" in her home.

_____

_____

RACHEL IN REMEMBRANCE

Rachel's death occurred during the birth of her second son, Benjamin (Genesis 35:18). Jacob placed a pillar on her grave in her memory.

Her memory, both beautiful and tragic, however, was to reach far beyond that grave on the way to Ephrath. She is certainly remembered for building the house of Israel (Ruth 4:11; Jeremiah 31:15; Matthew 2:18). For those who study her life, however, the beauty of what might have been is marred by the deception, envy, and idolatry that rendered her existence one of strife and unhappiness.

Let us glean from Rachel's example valuable lessons for our lives today:

❊Deception is always sinful and generally breeds misery.

❊God's plan for marriage was prescribed for the happiness of man and is still the only plan by which a marriage can attain the happiness which God intended for man and wife to share.

❅Envy is described as "rottenness to the bones" and is condemned in the New Testament.

❅A mere physical attraction does not automatically bring happiness in a marriage.

❅Idolatry is sinful in any form.

❅Idols reproduce.

❧ *Cindy's Reflections* ❧

Idol of the Heart

Have you bowed before an image
Carved of wood or filled with gold?
Did you promise your allegiance?
Did you offer up your soul?

It may be as days of pleasure
Turned to years of selfish pride,
You have slowly built a "golden calf"
And love for God has died.

You will find your "god" goes with you;
And you bow at his request.
He takes charge of your emotions;
And then robs you of your best.

Through the years you have enshrined him.
Now he can't be torn apart;
And the idol holds your future
For you built him in your heart.

Chapter 9

Serving from Second Place

Leah

Leah, one who lived her life in the shadow of another, faced many disabling limitations. She also was given numerous opportunities and blessings. Because she failed to find strength in trials, her opportunities for happiness always seemed to elude her.

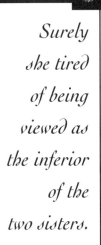

Surely she tired of being viewed as the inferior of the two sisters.

The Less-Beautiful Sister

In Genesis 29:17, Leah is introduced as being tender-eyed or as one having delicate eyes. This description likely means that her eyes were lacking in brilliance and luster. It is interesting to notice that, even in this brief introduction, she is compared to her beautiful sister Rachel. "Leah's eyes were delicate, but Rachel was beautiful of form and appearance" (Genesis 29:17). From this contrast, the fact that Leah was not exceedingly attractive is clearly indicated.

Likely, comparisons and contrasts between the two sisters were a never-ending discouragement to Leah. Surely she tired of being viewed as the inferior of the two sisters. Perhaps she, at times, felt ostracized because of her outward inadequacies. The limitations and problems that Leah faced can readily be seen.

There is, however, a right way and a wrong way to deal with any obstacle that fate may shove in my pathway. Perhaps if Leah had come to realize several things early in life, she could have avoided many heartaches and sorrows. Her life might have been fuller had she applied the following lessons to her own problem of being the less-beautiful sister:

❊*Some handicaps cannot be changed.* To every human is given some limitations. Each of us must realize that no one is gifted in every way. These natural limitations we must accept. They cannot be altered.

❊*Handicaps may be used as steppingstones.* Although handicaps, many times, cannot be overcome, they can overcome the lives of those they affect. They can also, however, be transformed into blessings when viewed as a source of strength. A weakness can teach one humility or embitter one's soul. A blindness can sharpen one's remaining senses or isolate one's life. A physical deformity may challenge one's mind or simply drown one in self-pity. We are told that some of Beethoven's greatest compositions were completed after he was deaf. The apostle Paul viewed his thorn in the flesh as a lesson in humility (2 Corinthians 12:7).

List your personal handicaps or limitations. Commit to pray for blessings of contentment as you overcome or accept these.

_____

_____

_____

Contentment can always be found. In Philippians 4:11, Paul said, "For I have learned in whatever state I am, to be content." Contentment for Paul meant a state of satisfaction and fulfillment in the face of persecutions, shipwreck, hunger, stoning, beatings, and even death. From his example we learn that true tranquility has little to do with one's lot in life or the outward conditions that may surround him. One must, on the other hand, rely on the living God, in trusting obedience, to overcome the hindrances that fate or circumstances may offer. Our prayer should be that we might know contentment in whatever state we may find ourselves.

Read 2 Corinthians 11:21–33 and list Paul's troubles. Keep this list on your refrigerator for one month as a "contentment reminder."

_____

_____

_____

God

grant me the

serenity to

accept the things I cannot change . . .

Courage to change those things I can,

And wisdom to know

the difference.

THE LESS-LOVED WIFE

Sadly enough, Leah's life was spent in pursuit of a goal that she could never attain. More than anything, she sought the abiding love and favor of her husband, Jacob. With each child she bore, Leah renewed her hope of being loved. Frustrated at her inability to win Jacob's eye, she resorted to spending her life in misery rather than looking for other sources of satisfaction and fulfillment. How many worthwhile accomplishments could have been attributed to the efforts of Leah if she had devoted herself to a full life of service to God and mankind! How sad is the plight of one who spends a lifetime grasping for the unreachable!

Goal-setting should be a part of the faithful Christian's life. Goals should be high, but within reach. Failure to reach a goal should not result in frustration, but in renewed zeal in accomplishments of new goals.

Examine your spiritual goal-setting habits. Do you:

✳write down long-term and short-term goals?

✳include personal study goals as well as evangelism goals?

✳keep your written goals in a prominent and frequented place?

✳pray about these goals regularly?

✳share these goals with another Christian when possible and ask for her prayers as you try to reach them?

✳re-examine and update them regularly?

THE UNGRATEFUL MOTHER

In Genesis 29:31 we are told that God opened the womb of Leah. The Lord saw that Jacob loved Leah little in comparison with his intense devotion to Rachel. Upon seeing this favoritism, God blessed Leah with children. She gave birth to four sons: Reuben, Simeon, Levi, and Judah. It seems that they brought little satisfaction, but rather were allowed by Leah simply to be the objects of further strife between the two sisters.

Since Rachel could bear no children at this time, she sent her handmaid in unto Jacob. After Rachel's handmaid Bilhah conceived, and almost as if a spiteful race for Jacob's affections was on, Leah sent her handmaid in unto Jacob, also. Zilpah, Leah's handmaid, gave birth to two sons, Gad and Asher. Leah's desire to win Jacob's love seemed to dominate all her thoughts and actions. She allowed God's blessing of children only to bring further contention.

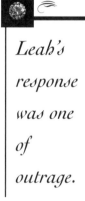

Leah's response was one of outrage.

Reuben, Leah's oldest son, likely about the age of four, went into the wheat fields during the time of harvest. While there, he gathered some yellow berries called mandrakes. The Hebrew root word for this fruit signifies love apples. The ancients believed that eating it would promote fertility. Some authorities say it has the effect of relaxing the womb.

At any rate, Reuben innocently brought the love fruit home. Rachel, the barren rival of his mother, asked for a portion of the mandrakes. Leah's response was one of outrage. In her anger she accused Rachel not only of stealing the mandrakes but also of stealing the affection of Jacob. This affection that she accused Rachel of stealing was likely something that Leah was never privileged to be given. She allowed her loneliness, in spite of the children God gave her, to tempt her to envy the love that Rachel was given and even to make accusations against Jacob's chosen bride, Rachel.

After eating the mandrakes, Leah conceived and gave birth to a son, Issachar. Later, Leah gave birth to another son and a daughter—Zebulun and Dinah.

The sons of Leah, later to grow into tribes of Israel, serve to remind us of the blessing Leah failed to appreciate. It was in the lineage of

Judah, her fourth son, that Christ was born. If Leah could have foreseen the coming of a Savior in her descendants, perhaps she would have received a measure of comfort. Leah's lesson for us today, however, is the importance of making the most of what we have—today.

Complete a list of the tribes of Israel according to the mother of each.

| Leah | Rachel | Bilhah | Zilpah |

⪻ *Cindy's Reflections* ⪼

Great Gifts

I prayed to God for strength anew
As I traveled life's rough road.
And I was told that strength belongs
To those who bear the load.

I asked the Lord for wisdom
In the judgments I must make.
And I was told to grasp it
From my failure or mistake.

I asked for faith that I could move
Great mountains for the Lord.
So God gave me the mountain
And the force was in His Word.

'Ere I yearn for some great gift
And raise my voice in prayer,
Remind me that great gifts are wrapped
In burdens I must bear.

CHAPTER 10

THE TROUBLE WITH SEXUAL SIN

DINAH

The story of Dinah begins shortly after the caravan of her father, Jacob, had arrived in the Shechem Valley. She was likely about fifteen years old as this tragic chapter in her life began to unfold.

Dinah "went out to see the daughters of the land."

A Shameful Sexual Sin

In Genesis 34:1 we read simply that Dinah, the daughter of Leah, "went out to see the daughters of the land." No further reason is given for Dinah's wandering in this land of strangers. Perhaps she, being the only sister among ten brothers, simply longed for the company of girls her own age. She may have merely been curious about the customs of her new environment. One historian tells us that she was attending a feast in Shechem. At any rate, we see her wandering, unattended, in a land of strangers.

The next verse tragically reveals that Dinah found much more adventure than she had ever intended. "And when Shechem the son of Hamor the Hivite, prince of the country, saw her, he took her and lay with her, and violated her" (Genesis 34:2).

From all indications, we understand from this verse that Dinah was raped. We are not given the details of either Shechem's advances or Dinah's reaction. Neither are we given any background information about the prince. Perhaps the fact that he was a Hivite prince caused him to feel that he was privileged to do as he pleased with unattended girls. We do see that Shechem was bent on seduction and thus accomplished his purpose. The key verse in regard to this sin is Genesis 34:7:

> And the sons of Jacob came in from the field when they heard it; and the men were grieved and very angry, because he had done a disgraceful thing in Israel by lying with Jacob's daughter, *a thing which ought not to be done* [emphasis added].

God does not view sex as evil. Remember, before sin entered the world God told Adam to "be fruitful and multiply; fill the earth" (Genesis 1:28). God's plan for the enjoyment of sex, however, is, and always has been, within the bonds of marriage: "Marriage is honorable among all, and the bed undefiled; but fornicators and adulterers God will judge"

(Hebrews 13:4). Any premarital or extramarital sexual act is a thing which ought not to be done.

We have no information as to whether Dinah was completely innocent or if, perhaps, she behaved in a way as to invite the ensuing trouble. It seems that she should have known that an unattended woman was considered legitimate prey by the men of Canaan (Genesis 12:15; 20:2; 26:7). To say the least, she should have been more cautious.

CAUTION TODAY

In our modern permissive society, the importance of being cautious cannot be overemphasized. One certainly does not have to be a prostitute to encourage and promote lust in a member of the opposite sex. Impurity in movement, immodesty in dress, or indiscretion in conversation can, correctly or not, be interpreted as an invitation to promiscuity. Certainly in a dating situation, participation in petting is dangerous. Petting by the unmarried is, in truth, illicit foreplay. In the marriage relationship, it arouses passions prior to intercourse. Heavy petting has been determined to have led to almost all teen pregnancies outside of marriage. Surely, as Christians we can see the dangers of stimulating such passions outside the bonds of marriage.

Certainly, responsibilities for the actions of a male, sexually aroused by an indiscriminate female, must rest on both partners. The Christian girl must be sure that her behavior is worthy of the Savior's name that she carries. Let us never be guilty of encouraging sexual sin.

Why is caution important for young women today?

What precautions, for example, should be taken by teens in your congregation or community to prevent the likelihood of sexual assault?

Discuss modest dress as a precautionary measure, along with discretion in conversation around guys.

A SHAMEFUL VENGEANCE

Even though the behavior of Shechem was abominable by any standards, he is described in Genesis 34:19 as being honorable. Perhaps it is this honor that motivated him to love and want to marry Dinah. His father, Hamor, approached Jacob in Shechem's behalf:

> "The soul of my son Shechem longs for your daughter. Please give her to him as a wife. And make marriages with us; give your daughters to us, and take our daughters to yourselves. So you shall dwell with us, and the land shall be before you. Dwell and trade in it, and acquire possessions for yourselves in it." Then Shechem said to her father and her brothers, "Let me find favor in your eyes, and whatever you say to me I will give" (Genesis 34:8–11).

Dinah's brothers refused to forgive and forget.

Hamor humbly offered to pay any price for Dinah and good relations with the family of Jacob. The brothers of Dinah, however, were not so willing to forgive and forget. They agreed to Hamor's plan if the men of the city would meet their terms: "But on this condition we will consent to you: If you will become as we are, if every male of you is circumcised" (Genesis 34:15).

In verse 24 we find that every male in the city was circumcised. This undoubtedly was an extremely painful ordeal for an adult, especially before the benefits of modern medicine were available.

Maliciously and cruelly, three days after the circumcisions, Dinah's brothers, Simeon and Levi, attacked the city, killing all the defenseless males. They stole all the city's valuables, even taking the wives and children of the murdered captives. This they did in the name of vengeance for Shechem's sin against their sister Dinah.

Simeon and Levi failed to realize that vengeance for sin belongs to God. "Beloved, do not avenge yourselves, but rather give place to wrath; for it is written, 'Vengeance is Mine, I will repay,' says the Lord" (Romans 12:19; cf. Deuteronomy 32:35).

Their idea of cruelly murdering the men of the city to repay the prince accomplished nothing for them, but most certainly inflicted God's wrath against them along with Shechem. In many ways their sin could be considered far worse than that of Shechem. Its consequences included the taking of many lives as well as inflicting grief and suffering on countless others.

Two wrongs never make a right.

> Read Romans 12:17-21. How do these verses teach us to treat those who may have wronged us?
>
> _____
>
> _____

A SHAMED FAMILY

It is astounding to think of the innocent lives that were taken or torn by Simeon and Levi on this occasion. One man committed a sexual sin, and these brothers avenged his sin by taking many lives, leaving widows and fatherless children. The price tag for the innocent was extremely high.

So many times today people fool themselves into thinking that their sin is their business. Parents hear young people reason, "It's my life to ruin." Is it really just my business if I decide to sin, or will innocent people likely be hurt? Is it really only my life I am ruining, or am I causing sorrow in the lives of others? Am I hurting those who taught me the difference between right and wrong? Can I really pay the price—alone? Simeon and Levi could not.

> Then Jacob said to Simeon and Levi, "You have troubled me by making me obnoxious among the inhabitants of the land, among the Canaanites and the Perizzites; and since I am few in number, they will gather themselves together against me and kill me. I shall be destroyed, my household and I" (Genesis 34:30).

The reputation of Jacob's family had been destroyed by two of its members. When considering the results of sin, the shame it may bring on others should be carefully contemplated.

> What sins always negatively affect innocent people?
>
> _____
>
> List other biblical examples of innocent people who suffered as a result of the sins of others; then discuss examples from the lives of class members?
>
> _____
>
> _____

∞ *Cindy's Reflections* ∞

Version #1

If You Love Me, You Will

by Will D. Stroyer

If you love me you will. You will forget all of the no nonsense stuff your mom and dad have taught you . . . All that kid stuff you learned in Sunday school. That's not the real world. The real world is you coming to the prom with me. Look, this is the only time I'll ever be a senior and you are the one I want to be with. I know you love me and I know you will.

If you love me you will. Look, I'm not asking you to be a bad person or anything. I'm just asking you to go to a movie that everybody's going to see. It's a number one movie. It's not like it's pornographic or anything. So what are a few bad words and a few sex scenes? Just because we see it doesn't mean we approve of it. It's just the real world. Come on and loosen up a little for me. I know you care about me. You will, won't you?

If you love me you will. Just because you go with me to the party doesn't mean you have to drink. But, hey, I can't ask all these guys to stop doing what they've always done or I can't just stop being friends with them because of us. I love you more than life and I know you love me, too. I'll be sure to make sure no one makes fun of you. Come on and be with me. Maybe you can even help my friends be better. They sure do need friends like you. If you love me, you will.

If you love me you will. I'm not asking you to actually have sex. But let's face it. Everybody spends time alone getting to know each other. Everybody kisses, I mean really kisses and I love every part of you. Don't you love me, too? Don't you want to be close and intimate with me? I'm not talking about going all the way. What I'm talking about is just a natural part of being in love. Most people don't even discuss it . . . they just do it. If you love me, you will.

If you love me you will. After all it's been a long time now. We've come over so many hurdles. Neither of us could stand going on without the other. We know we're not breaking up. Besides, what is such a big deal about sex anyway? We're more in love than all of our friends who are obviously having sex at least on the weekends. They even talk about it. I think they already assume we do, and by now we aren't risking anything at all . . . in fact we're just getting ready for the life together that we both are counting on. I believe you love me with all your heart and I know you want me to be happy. If you love me, you will.

⇒◆⇐

Version #2

If You Love Me, You Will

by Ima Faith Walker

If you love me, you will. You will respect me so much that you will respect my parents. You will speak gently and with kindness to them and about them. You will never ask me to do anything that would bring shame to them or violate their trust in me. You will genuinely care about all I care about. If you love me, you will.

If you love me, you will. You will shield me from those things that might be offensive to me. You will never put a stumbling block in my way to heaven. You will choose for us activities that are good for both of our reputations. You will pray with me. You will realize the value of my soul and you will always put me on a pedestal, never even asking me to do anything that would violate my conscience. You will help me to go to heaven. If you love me, you will.

If you love me, you will. You will demand that I associate with those who are good influences. You will never ask me to be a part of a crowd that enjoys drinking or offensive forms of entertainment. You will never place your friendships above my honor. You will only have one who means more to you than I do. God will be supreme in your heart and I will be second. You will be willing to sacrifice all relationships that would disappoint your heavenly Father. If you love me, you will.

If you love me, you will. You will want me to wear clothing that is not skin tight, low cut, too short, or too revealing, because you are saving me for a time when we might begin our lives as husband and wife. You are aware that your purity of mind can be forfeited by a lustful look, so you will avoid situations in which you might be tempted to lust. You will avoid pornographic materials and places where women are usually not wearing enough clothes. You will never ask me to dance, to touch you in any impure way, or even talk to me in sexually explicit terms, because you love me and want me to walk in the light of God's love. You will never ask or expect anything of me that will cause me the pain of regret later on, but instead you will do anything to help me have a happy marriage one day. If you love me, you will.

If you love me, you will demand that our relationship has no secrets. It will be an open book before our parents, before our friends, and before our God. You will do anything to keep it this way. You will want to make of our bodies living sacrifices, holy and acceptable. If you love me, you will.

———⟫·◇·⟪———

Version #3

If You Love Me, You Will

Jesus Christ

If you love Me . . . keep my commandments

— (John 14:15; cf. 14:23)

Who loves you?

Whom do you love?

Which version are you reading?

Which version are you writing?

CHAPTER 11

WHEN LIFE ISN'T FAIR

TAMAR

In the story of Tamar, we find a combination of unfortunate circumstances and corrupt characters that together produced a succession of hideous sins.

THE WIDOW

We know nothing of the background of Tamar. She appeared first when Judah chose her to be the wife of Er, his oldest son. This in itself proved to be the first of several sour relationships in the life of Tamar. The Scriptures describe Er as being "wicked" (Genesis 38:7) and add that "the Lord killed him," thus widowing young Tamar.

According to the prevailing levirate law, Onan, the second son of Judah, was bound to marry Tamar. He did so, and the following description is given of this relationship: "But Onan knew that the heir would not be his; and it came to pass, when he went in to his brother's wife, that he emitted on the ground, lest he should give an heir to his brother" (Genesis 38:9).

Obviously, Onan had no intention of raising seed to his brother as the law required. Thus, God was displeased with him also, and took his life as well. Tamar was once again both husbandless and childless.

One third son, Shelah, remained in the house of Judah. Legally he was required to marry Tamar. Judah asked Tamar to remain single and wait for Shelah.

> Then Judah said to Tamar his daughter-in-law, "Remain a widow in your father's house till my son Shelah is grown." For he said, "Lest he also die like his brothers." And Tamar went and dwelt in her father's house (Genesis 38:11).

Tamar was husbandless and childless.

According to the prevailing levirate law, Onan, the second son of JudAt first glance it seems that Judah simply wanted Tamar to wait for Shelah to mature before their marriage took place. A careful examination of this verse, however, reveals that Judah was hesitant to let Shelah marry Tamar. Note his apprehension in the words, "Lest he also die like his brothers." It becomes clear that Judah viewed Tamar as the bearer of bad luck. He actually blamed Tamar for the deaths of his two sons. He failed to realize that his sons brought death upon themselves by the wicked deeds they committed. Is it not easy for us today to lay the guilt of sin upon innocent shoulders? It is always hard to find fault in the lives of those we love.

What often happens when parents attempt to justify or excuse negative behavior on the part of their children?

_____

_____

Give examples of how this might hamper the spiritual growth of these children.

_____

Tamar—widowed, abused, and rejected—now must face life alone. In the most miserable of circumstances she is now forced to begin again. As was evidenced in the life of Leah, even life's lowest ebb can be transformed into an opportunity to glorify God. Tragically, Tamar rejected this opportunity and all principles of righteousness.

THE HARLOT

With the passing of time, Tamar's loneliness deepened, turning into bitterness. Perhaps she grew to resent the family of Judah who left her wearing the dismal garments of widowhood and feeling the lonely pangs of childlessness.

Tamar, however, was not alone for long in her widowhood. The wife of Judah, her father-in-law, passed away. Thus Judah was alone also. The season of sheep shearing approached. This was traditionally a time of jovial festivities—a time of excessive drinking. Judah apparently became involved in the festivities, for he owned sheep.

When Tamar heard that Judah was in Timnah for the occasion, she devised a deceitful plan. She put aside her garments of widowhood and disguised herself as a harlot. She then cleverly placed herself in an entranceway in Timnah. She was determined, regardless of cost, to bear children of the family of Judah.

The trap was set, and Judah plunged into it. Since Tamar was veiled, he was ignorant of the fact that the harlot was his daughter-in-law. He agreed to pay her a kid from his flock for sexual submission.

The deal was made. The sin of incest was committed. Tamar's plan, however, was not complete. She wanted proof that Judah had committed the sin of whoredom. Since the kid was to be delivered later in payment, she asked for a pledge, or some collateral, to insure that Judah would pay. She craftily asked him to leave his seal, cord, and staff. The seal was likely a ring or cylinder seal attached to Judah's person by a cord. The staff was probably delicately carved. All of these things were distinctively Judah's and could easily be identified as belonging to him.

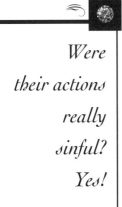

Were their actions really sinful? Yes!

Of course, when the kid of payment arrived, there was no harlot to be found. A mourning widow had cleverly taken her place.

Tamar had been handed a raw deal by Judah's family. She really was entitled to children by Judah's family. Judah was alone in life and did not intend to commit incest. In this situation, then, were their actions really sinful? The answer, of course, is yes!

Many today advocate that the sinfulness of the act depends on the situation surrounding it. This false idea has become known as situation ethics. This concept is nowhere found in the Scripture. God's laws are always applicable. Sin is always sin. There is no such thing as a good reason for sin. (Read 2 Samuel 6:6–7.)

The Mother

Tamar's scheme went as planned. She did, indeed, conceive by Judah. The news of Tamar's pregnancy spread quickly. When it reached the ears of Judah, he was outraged. As the leader of his family, he ordered her to be burned.

Tamar was prepared for this consequence. She had three very important pieces of evidence that pointed to the identity of the father. They pointed directly to Judah. His guilt was unmistakably obvious. He, thus, acknowledged that his sin was even greater than that of Tamar: "So Judah acknowledged them and said, 'She has been more righteous than I, because I did not give her to Shelah my son.' And he never knew her again" (Genesis 38:26).

The time of delivery came for Tamar, and she bore twins. The delivery is described in Genesis 38:27–30 as an unusual one. The twins were named Perez and Zerah. The children that she had deeply desired now lived to remind both Tamar and Judah of their sinful past.

> Of what significance was a scarlet thread in the life of Tamar?
>
> _____

Christians who have lived long enough know that God can make good come even from situations brought about by evil. So when we determine to avoid deceit and vengeance in our lives, good results from Tamar's evil. A very good man was born into Tamar's family through her illegitimate son Perez. His name was Joseph and he was a carpenter in Nazareth (Matthew 1:3–16).

> Find Tamar's name in Matthew chapter 1. How did God, in this instance, use evil for His bigger purpose?
>
> _____
>
> What other women are listed in the lineage of Christ?
>
> _____
>
> Which of these, like Tamar, had a blatant sin in her life?
>
> _____

※Sin is still sin even when it appears in the lives of those we love most (2 Samuel 18:33).

※An opportunity to glorify God can always be found even in the face of adversity (1 Corinthians 10:13).

※"What a tangled web we weave, when first we practice to deceive" (cf. Proverbs 20:17).

※God can bring good even from sinful situations.

⇌ *Cindy's Reflections* ⇋

Count It All Joy

It's not that trials pass me by
And leave me unaffected;
For I have felt the pain of loss
And I have been rejected.

The storms of life have gathered round
And filled my life with sorrow;
And I, too, have looked hopelessly
At prospects of tomorrow.

Heartaches come to everyone
And, finally, all will die.
The difference for His children is . . .
Our Father tells us why.

The trials make us stronger
For the crosses that we bear;
And fit us for the kingdom
He's preparing for us there.

They give us more compassion
For another soul that bleeds.
They teach us how to empathize
And fill a brother's needs.

They tell us of our wretchedness
When we're without the Lord.
They teach us to depend on Him
And hope for His reward.

For those without the promises
The trials bring naught but pain.
But we can count it all but joy
For heaven's ours to gain.

CHAPTER 12

THE EVIL TEMPTRESS

POTIPHAR'S WIFE

Nothing good can be said of Potiphar's wife. She was evil personified as she entered Joseph's life. She became an integral part of God's good plan, however, for Joseph's life. "All things work together for good to those who love God, to those who are the called according to His purpose" (Romans 8:28).

Potiphar's wife became a walking, talking temptation.

THE HUMAN TEMPTATION

Throughout history, God has expected His people to be tempted. Each day those of us who serve Him must face the constant enticement of Satan to engage in that which is evil. The fact that temptation plagues man universally is evidenced throughout the pages of Holy Writ (1 Corinthians 10:12–13; Galatians 6:1). Notice that even Christ met with temptation during His life on earth. "For we do not have a High Priest who cannot sympathize with our weaknesses, but was in all points tempted as we are, yet without sin" (Hebrews 4:15).

God expects man to be tempted. There are those, however, who not only fall prey to temptation but also choose to be the tempters. They, by the lives they live, serve as a daily temptation to those about them. God's people, though tempted, should never allow themselves to be used as Satan's tool to tempt others. Notice how Potiphar's wife became to Joseph a walking, talking temptation. "And it came to pass after these things that his master's wife cast longing eyes on Joseph, and she said, 'Lie with me'" (Genesis 39:7).

Joseph had recently been sold as a slave into Egypt by his brothers. It seems that even in these, the worst of conditions, Joseph had proved himself honest and industrious and thus had risen to a place of distinction. He had been given the position of overseer in the house of the ruler Potiphar. His ability and integrity were unquestioned by his superior. Potiphar had entrusted his all into the hands of Joseph. There was another, however, in whom Potiphar could not afford to place any degree of trust.

In Genesis 39:6 we are told that "Joseph was handsome in form and appearance." Hebrew scholars tell us that this, in modern terms, could be translated "well built and good looking."

It was by this man, superior in person and personality, that Potiphar's wife was tempted. Perhaps many women in her position would have been tempted just as she was. The tragedy of the account is not that she was tempted, but that she first fell to the temptation and then allowed herself to tempt another with the words, "Lie with me" (Genesis 39:7).

> In what seemingly innocent situations may we find ourselves which, if left unchecked, may lead to adultery?
>
> _____
>
> What personal rules can married women set for ourselves that may help eliminate any temptation to commit adultery? Add to this list:

❄Don't go to lunch alone with other men.

❄Abstain from conversation about intimate issues with other men.

❄Enjoy hobbies and take vacations with your husband.

❄Keep your home and computer completely free from pornography.

❄ _____

PROGRESSIVE SIN

If a person jumps from the top of a three-story building, he would likely receive quite a jolt. However, should the same person go down the same three stories on a ladder step by step, he would hardly notice the descension at all. Satan realizes that this same principle applies to sin. Generally speaking, people do not suddenly plunge headlong into heinous sin. Rather, they slip gradually, one sin at a time, into Satan's grasp. The alcoholic becomes such, one drink at a time. The non-attending Christian becomes such by missing one service at a time. The point is obvious. Sin works progressively in our lives.

Notice the progression of sin in the life of Potiphar's wife:

❄She cast longing eyes upon Joseph (v. 7).

※She said, "Lie with me" (v. 7).

※She spoke to Joseph day by day (v. 10).

※She caught him by his garment, saying, "Lie with me" (v. 12).

※She lied to the men of the house (vv. 14–15).

※She lied to her husband (vv. 16–18).

In the First Psalm we see another illustration of the progression of sin. Notice the progression of verse 1: first the walking, then the standing, and finally the sitting. "Blessed is the man who *walks* not in the counsel of the ungodly, nor *stands* in the path of sinners, nor *sits* in the seat of the scornful [emphasis added]" (Psalm 1:1).

Satan is clever. He often succeeds in turning the best of men into his servants—one step at a time.

ADULTERY: A THREEFOLD SIN

It is not unusual to hear sins classified or categorized. For example, one sin may be referenced as a mild sin while another, a worse sin, and still another, a terrible sin. Classifying sin, within itself, is a mistake, for God views every sin as an abomination.

While grouping sins according to their "badness" is not in keeping with the Scriptures, certainly the Scriptures show that the consequences of some sins are far worse than those of others. Common sense will lead us to the same conclusion. If a person is guilty of entertaining an evil thought, for instance, he has sinned against God. If a person, however, is guilty of murder, he has not only sinned against God but also against the murdered and those who grieve for him. The consequences of the latter sin are graver than those of the former.

Adultery is a sin of far-reaching consequences. When tempted, Joseph was able to see these consequences. Notice his response.

> Look, my master does not know what is with me in the house, and he has committed all that he has to my hand. There is no one greater in this house than I, nor has he kept back anything from me but you, because you are his wife. How then can I do this great wickedness, and sin against God? (Genesis 39:8–9).

First, Joseph realized that adultery was a sin against the innocent marriage partner. His words, "nor has he kept back anything from me," show that he resisted the temptation on Potiphar's account. When a person engages in sexual activity with a married person, he sins against the spouse of that person.

Second, Joseph knew that adultery, in this case, would have been a sin against Potiphar's wife. He understood her marriage caused her to be "kept back" from him. Adultery is a sin against the person with whom it is committed.

Third and foremost, Joseph asked, "How then can I do this great wickedness, and sin against God?" Adultery is a sin against God.

Name another sin that is comparatively great in its consequences.

_____

PERSISTENCE IN SIN

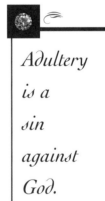

Someone has wisely said, "No one has ever drowned from going under water, but from staying there."

Potiphar's wife was persistent in her effort to commit sexual sin with Joseph. Verse 10 tells us that she spoke to Joseph day by day.

Repentance from sin invokes the forgiveness of God on the sinner, removing all guilt. But there is no forgiveness for one who persists in sin.

Adultery is a sin against God.

HIDING SIN WITH MORE SIN

Throughout the Bible, we see examples of people who attempted to hide sin. In the beginning, Adam and Eve attempted to hide, even from God, after the first sin (Genesis 3). David murdered in an attempt to hide his adultery with Bathsheba (2 Samuel 11). Potiphar's wife also attempted to hide sin with more sin.

When Joseph daily refused to submit to the temptation of Potiphar's wife, she "caught him by his garment, saying, 'Lie with me.'" Joseph, determined to be faithful to Potiphar and God, ran from the room, leaving his garment in her hand.

Notice Joseph's defense against sexual temptation. Why is a quick exit the appropriate response rather than talking it out or praying together about the temptation?

_____

_____

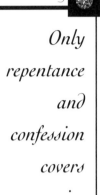

Only repentance and confession covers sin.

Potiphar's wife, realizing that she would be under great suspicion, quickly raised an outcry against Joseph to divert attention to him:

> See, he has brought in to us a Hebrew to mock us. He came in to me to lie with me, and I cried out with a loud voice. And it happened, when he heard that I lifted my voice and cried out, that he left his garment with me, and fled and went outside (Genesis 39:14–15).

Potiphar's wife shamelessly used deception to cover her attempted adultery. Although sin may be hidden to the eyes of man, only repentance and confession can truly cover sin with the mercy of God. "He who covers his sins will not prosper, but whoever confesses and forsakes them will have mercy" (Proverbs 28:13).

Go back through this book and list the incidents involving deception. Begin with Satan's deceit in lesson 1. In how many of the occurrences did the deception result in additional sin?

_____

_____

Give examples from recent history or court cases in which men or women have fruitlessly attempted to hide sin with more sin.

_____

PERSECUTION FOR RIGHTEOUSNESS' SAKE

"Then Joseph's master took him and put him into the prison, a place where the king's prisoners were confined. And he was there in the prison" (Genesis 39:20). As a result of Joseph's integrity and righteousness in the face of temptation, he was cast into prison. God does not promise that a life of service to Him will be easy. Often those who are faithful will find themselves encountering persecutions as a result of their faith. Notice in Genesis 41:41, however, that Joseph had not only regained his freedom, but had also gained rule over the kingdom of Egypt.

There are those today who are persecuted for righteousness' sake. To these Christians is promised the kingdom as well. "Blessed are those who are persecuted for righteousness' sake, for theirs is the kingdom of heaven" (Matthew 5:10).

Cindy's Reflections

When the last line has been written
And my time on earth is through,
What will my friends remember
When they see my empty pew?

Will they say I've gone to glory
And declare with certainty?
Or wonder if His grace is vast
Enough for even me?

Will they say, "This church will miss
Her great example to our youth"?
Will they say I led them heavenward
If they really tell the truth?

What of my home and family?
If I reach my present goals,
Will I leave behind a spotless house
Or blood-cleansed spotless souls?

My legacy for others . . .
Just what's on the bottom line?
If it's figured all in dollars
I'll leave every cent behind.

But if my kids' inheritance
Is faith and purity,
Then they are very rich! My
Legacy will follow me!

CHAPTER 13

SALT IN HIS WOUND

JOB'S WIFE

There has been much controversy regarding the book of Job. Many scholars believe that Job lived during the pre-Mosaic period around the time of the life of Abraham. For this reason we include Job's wife in *Women of the Genesis*.

A FINAL EXAMINATION

Testing has become a part of the American way of life. It seems that in our society, success is often measured by one's ability to pass a test. Throughout school, students are assigned grades based on their performance on various examinations. Often, job applicants are required to pass an exam before being considered for a position. The ultimate test, that test which really does determine success or failure, was given in the book of Job. Job successfully passed this extreme and final examination. Sadly though, his wife failed in every aspect.

In the first chapter of Job, we are introduced to a very unusual man. He, being described as the greatest man in the East, was the owner of sheep, oxen, donkeys, and camels, animals numbering 11,500 in all. Along with this great wealth, he had been blessed with ten children. This very prosperous man had not allowed his riches to interfere with his service to God. Notice the Lord's commendation of Job: "There is none like him on the earth, a blameless and upright man, one who fears God and shuns evil" (Job 1:8).

Is it wrong to be wealthy? Give Bible examples of wealthy people who pleased God and wealthy people who did not. Discuss the difference.

_____

_____

What makes wealth a blessing? What makes it a curse?

_____

_____

God was very proud of His servant Job and even exhibited him to Satan as an example of a true servant of the Lord. Satan, in his typical contemptible manner, had this reply to the Lord's commendation of Job:

Does Job fear God for nothing? Have You not made a hedge around him, around his household, and around all that he has on every side? You have blessed the work of his hands, and his possessions have increased in the land. But now, stretch out Your hand and touch all that he has, and he will surely curse You to Your face! (Job 1:9–11).

Satan always takes advantage of every opportunity to tempt mankind. He believed that Job's service to God was a sort of "fair weather" service. He was sure that Job would curse God if his many blessings were taken from him. God allowed Satan to test the faith of Job by taking his possessions and his family. Thus, for Job, the ultimate test began.

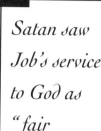

Satan saw Job's service to God as "fair weather service."

It seems that of all the types of tests that are daily administered, that test for which one has no chance to prepare is the most difficult. In high school such an exam is called a pop test. Job's test was, in a manner of speaking, a pop test. Notice all of the sudden surprises that Mr. and Mrs. Job faced in one disastrous day:

* All of the oxen and donkeys were stolen (vv. 14–15).

* Some of the servants were murdered with the sword (vv. 15).

* All of the sheep were burned to death (v. 16).

* Some of the servants were burned to death (v. 16).

* The camels were stolen (v. 17).

* All of the children were killed in a storm (v. 18–19).

GOOD VS. ADVERSITY

Imagine the impact of living through a day such as this one in the life of Job! It seems that every imaginable evil had touched his life. In one day his life had changed from that of being the wealthiest man in the land to a most sorrowful pauper. His attitude toward the Lord, however, remained the same. "In all this Job did not sin nor charge God with wrong" (Job 1:22).

As one might expect, Satan was not satisfied with Job's reaction. He attributed Job's faithfulness to the fact that his physical health and life had not been endangered. Thus, God allowed Satan to try Job further. "So Satan went out from the presence of the Lord, and struck Job with painful boils from the sole of his foot to the crown of his head" (Job 2:7).

Job's existence was reduced to one of pain and misery. His faith had been tried to an extreme degree. The sincerity of his motives and the purity of his devotion could not be questioned. Notice Job's words: "'Shall we indeed accept good from God, and shall we not accept adversity?' In all this Job did not sin with his lips" (Job 2:10).

In all this, Job did not sin with his lips.

Mrs. Job, like her husband, had been tested. Her children, her wealth, and the health of her husband had all suddenly been snatched away. Her tragic failure to prove her faith is seen in Job 2:9: "Do you still hold fast to your integrity? Curse God and die!"

We know nothing good about Job's wife. From this statement we know that she fell spiritually, with the great material fall of Job's house. Truly she failed the test.

She Failed to Realize the Sovereignty of God.

There are only two great forces in the world. God and good are in constant opposition to Satan and evil. Many times throughout history, for a brief moment, Satan and evil have appeared to conquer. This would certainly be the case at this point in the life of Job. How desperate the circumstances must have appeared to Mrs. Job as she looked upon her husband as he scraped the infected sores with a broken piece of pottery in search of relief. It was at this nauseating moment that Mrs. Job lost sight of the sovereignty of God. She failed to realize that Jehovah reigns supreme, and His power is sufficient to conquer all. Her faith in the God who is "able to deliver" (Daniel 3:17) wavered, and suddenly she became the devil's advocate, hurling at Job the most devastating blow he was to face. His one remaining encouragement was transformed into his greatest trial.

Today, as Christians, we must base our lives on the fact that God is able to deliver. On one dismal day, the sun actually did refuse to shine. The fear of this tragic day was seen in the trembling of the earth itself. A Savior died. For this, another brief moment of history, Satan and evil seemed to prevail.

In this, the most somber instant in all the ages, Christ arose. In this victorious resurrection, Satan and death were forever conquered. This victory empowers Christians today to triumph over any blow that Satan may hurl. We, unlike Job's wife, in times of trial must have the foresight to see that God will deliver and doubly bless in the end (Job 42:10). "Yet in all these things we are more than conquerors through Him who loved us" (Romans 8:37).

Read Daniel chapter 3. Under what circumstances did Shadrach, Meshach and Abednego say their God was able?

Read the "victory verses" in Romans 8:31–39. Include verse 37 in a card of encouragement to a sick or troubled sister this week. Write words or phrases below that give you strength.

She Failed to Give Support to Her Godly Husband.

In Genesis 2 when woman was created, her purpose was clearly stated: "I will make him a helper comparable to him" (Genesis 2:18). Job's wife sadly failed in her duty to encourage her husband in his time of greatest need.

Many times today, godly men must fight a constant battle at home before they can begin to wage their war against sin in the world. How tragic it is to see would-be leaders in God's kingdom restrained by the weakness of modern day "Mrs. Jobs." Administrators in today's training schools for preachers tell us that much of a student's success is dependent on the attitude of his wife. Let us be careful to encourage the worthy endeavors of our righteous mates. Seldom will a man become greater than his wife will allow him to become.

Trials serve to help strengthen the inner man.

SHE FAILED TO SEEK STRENGTH IN TRIALS.

The trials that Job's wife suffered were, by any standard, extreme. The loss of possessions, children, and her husband's health were no doubt devastating. Her response to suffering was to abandon her faith in God.

Like Job's wife, many Christians believe that one's material circumstance in life is directly related to his relationship to God. Many times people even force themselves into needless guilt in an attempt to explain the tribulations they face.

Hebrews 12:6 tells us that "whom the Lord loves he chastens." Verse 10 of the same chapter even states that this chastening is for our profit. Notice how various trials may be profitable to the faithful Christian:

❊ The loss of material wealth shows the Christian the unstable nature of the world's treasures and the fallacy of trusting in them. (Read Matthew 6:19–21.)

❊ The loss of loved ones is a lesson in the temporary nature of life itself. In times of such grief, the Christian sees the importance of preparing for eternity. (Read 1 Corinthians 15:54–55.)

❊ Physical illness to the children of God is a reminder of our dependence on God. Our helplessness without Him manifests itself in times of sickness. (Read 2 Kings 20:1–3.)

❊ Discouragement or disappointment from those around us should be a strong incentive for the Christian to draw nigh to the One who will never leave nor forsake us. (Read Hebrews 13:5.)

Trials not only serve to help strengthen the inner man, but also can be used by the Christian as a tool to help others. When those about us need comfort and sympathy, those Christians who have experienced the pangs of suffering are able to extend that needed hand of sympathy.

Why do you think Satan allowed Mrs. Job to live when he caused the other family members to perish?

_____

It has been said that trials neither make nor break a person. They only show what he really is. Job's wife, when put to the test, was found wanting. Careful consideration should be given in our lives to this same test. Could you pass this ultimate test of your faith? "If you faint in the day of adversity, your strength is small" (Proverbs 24:10)

Find the "conclusion of the whole matter" in Ecclesiastes 12. How does the "fear of the Lord" and "keeping His commandments" add peace and contentment to our lives?

_____

How does Romans 8:28 factor into this peace in troubled times?

_____

⇒ *Cindy's Reflections* ⇒

Let This Cup Pass

Let this cup pass from me, O Lord,
This burden is too great.
But I learned perseverance
As He taught my soul to wait.

I was lost in all my blessings
And caught up in daily living,
But my cup of sorrow showed me
Truths in gratitude and giving.

I thought that I was in control
'Til trials made me see
I am nothing by myself,
For it's Christ who strengthens me.

I yearned for something better
With each sorrow that was hurled,
And I found my hope grow stronger
For a new and better world.

So stripped of pride and earth's stains
In this lifetime's darkest day,
My soul had learned submission
And my heart had learned to pray.

My cup has changed to blessing
But please let me not forget
That until I bless another,
I'm not finished with it yet.

Let this cup pass, O Father,
But not until I drink
In the stillness of the night
Teach me, Father, make me think.